Apples of Gold

Compiled by John R. Ric

D1526952

Copyright, January, 1960, by
SWORD OF THE LORD FOUNDATION
ISBN 0-87398-017-4
Renewal 1988

SWORD of the LORD
PUBLISHERS
P.O.BOX 1099, MURFREESBORO, TN 37133

Printed in U. S. A.

ACKNOWLEDGEMENTS

The author and publisher wish to give grateful thanks to the following for permission to reprint these copyrighted poems and other selections:

"All Your Anxiety," by E. H. Joy. Copyright 1946 by Alfred B. Smith in *Favorites, Vol. 2.* Assigned to Singspiration, Inc. Used by permission.

"Counted Worthy," and "Sometimes," by Annie Johnson Flint. Copyright. Reproduced by permission Evangelical Publishers, Toronto, Canada.

"Home," by Edgar A. Guest, from the book, *Living the Years--All in a Life Time,* copyright 1949 by the Reilly & Company, Chicago.

"If I Could Choose My Way," by Avis B. Christiansen, from *His Faithfulness,* published by Loizeaux Brothers, New York.

"What Is Prayer?" by James Montgomery, and "The Sentinel," by James G. Lawson, from *Best Loved Religious Poems,* published by Fleming H. Revell Company, Westwood, New Jersey.

"A Prayer for Courage," by Grace Noll Crowell, from the book, *Flame in the Wind.* Copyright 1930 & 34, and "Promised Strength," by Grace Noll Crowell, from, *Apples of Gold.* Copyright 1950. Reproduced by permission Harper and Brothers, New York.

"Bible Study," "Anticipation," "My Advocate," "Suppose," by Martha Snell Nicholson. Copyright by Moody Press Chicago. Used by permission.

"The Fountain of Life," by A. B. Simpson. Permission has been granted by Christian Publications, Inc., New York.

"Devotion," by Henry W. Frost. Used by permission China Inland Mission, Philadelphia.

"The Lord Giveth," "Watch Yourself Go By," by Strickland Gillilan, from the book, *Gillilan, Finnigin & Co.,* published by the Rodeheaver Hall-Mack Co., Chicago. Used by permission.

*   *   *

Our sincere appreciation to the following authors for the use of their poems in this book:

Ada Blankhorn, Benton T. Bradley, Ophelia Browning, John Burton, E. Margaret Clarkson, Eva Gray, Bob Jones, Jr. Edith M. Lee, Albert Leighton, Emma A. Lent, A. M. Overton, Barbara C. Ryberg, Margaret Sangster, Robert E. Sells, Robert P. Shuler, Oswald J. Smith, Helen Welshimer, Amos R. Wells, Margaret Wendel, Margaret Widdemer, Julia W. Wolfe.

Earnest effort has been made to secure permission from authors and owners for the use of their material. Any errors that may have possibly been made are unintentional and will be corrected in future printings if the publisher is notified.

INTRODUCTION

The blessed Word of God says, "A word fitly spoken is like apples of gold in pictures of silver" (Prov. 25:11).

So, in our memories we should store beautiful thoughts, stated in beautiful words. Poetry has a charm for the memory. Rythm, rhyme, alliteration, parallelism, and contrast, all help us to remember beautiful thoughts. Christmas presents are more enjoyable for pretty wrappings. Many a wonderful thought can be better received, remembered and taught with a poem.

So here I have selected some of the best poems for enjoyment and use of Christians. Many of them have been used in THE SWORD OF THE LORD with great blessing, and I hope they may prove heart warming and blessed to thousands of others.

John R. Rice

The Bible

FIRST BIBLE

A little boy's first Bible
Is the greatest thrill he's known;
There's a sweet, unique excitement
In a Bible all his own!
And yet my heart is smitten
As this touching sight I see--
Has his reverence for that Bible
Depended much on me?
As I see him with his Bible,
I bow my head and pray--
May he always love that Bible
The way he does today.
Then I hear a voice within me
Speak in solemn words and true;
How he cherishes that Bible
Will depend a lot on you!
I love my Bible better
Since I've seen the beaming joy
This wonderful possession
Has afforded to my boy.
May I seek to give mine daily
A devotion he can see,
For the love he bears his Bible
Will depend a lot on me.

--United Presbyterian

BIBLE STUDY

Would it not be a foolish thing
To die of thirst, with this clear spring
Of living water at my feet?
To starve when there is bread and meat
And wine before me on the board,
A table spread by my dear Lord?
And would we think he has much sense
Who hoarded only copper pence,
When at his feet, and all around
Were diamonds sparkling on the ground?

--Martha Snell Nicholson

I am always suspicious of profound explanations of Scripture, explanations that require a scholar or philosopher to understand them. The Bible is a plain man's book (Matt.11:25). In at least ninety-nine cases in a hundred the meaning of Scripture lies on the surface--the meaning that any simple-minded man, woman, or child who really wants to know and obey the truth would see in it. *R. A. Torrey*

MY MOTHER'S BIBLE

This book is all that's left me now,
Tears will unbidden start;
With faltering lip and throbbing brow
I press it to my heart.
For many generations past,
Here is our family tree;
My mother's hand this Bible clasped;
She, dying, gave it to me.

Ah! well do I remember those
Whose names these records bear,
Who 'round the hearthstone used to close
After the evening prayer
And speak of what these pages said,
In tones my heart would thrill!
Though they are with the silent dead,
Here they are living still!

My father read this Holy Book
To brothers, sisters, dear;
How calm was my poor mother's look
Who loved God's Word to hear.
Her angel face--I see it yet!
What thronging memories come!
Again that little group is met
Within the halls of home!

Thou truest friend man ever knew,
Thy constancy I've tried;
Where all were false I found thee true!
My counselor and guide.
The mines of earth no treasure give
That could this volume buy;
In teaching me the way to live,
It taught me how to die.

--George Morris

CLING TO THE BIBLE

Cling to the Bible, though all else be taken;
Lose not its promises precious and sure;
Souls that are sleeping, its echoes awaken,
Drink from the fountain, so peaceful, so pure.

Cling to the Bible, this jewel, this treasure
Brings to us honor and saves fallen man;
Pearl whose great value no mortal can measure,
Seek and secure it, O soul, while you can.

Lamp for the feet that in byways have wandered,
Guide for the youth that would otherwise fall;
Hope for the sinner whose best days are squandered,
Staff for the aged, and best Book of all.

—M. J. Smith

Character

ELEGY WRITTEN IN A COUNTRY CHURCH-YARD
(condensed form)

Beneath those rugged elms, that yew-tree's shade,
  Where heaves the turf in many a mould'ring heap,
Each in his narrow cell forever laid,
  The rude forefathers of the hamlet sleep.

Let not ambition mock their useful toil,
  Their homely joys, and destiny obscure;
Nor grandeur hear with a disdainful smile
  The short and simple annals of the poor.

The boast of heraldry, the pomp of power,
  And all that beauty, all that wealth e'er gave,
Awaits alike the inevitable hour:
  The paths of glory lead but to the grave.

Nor you, ye proud, impute to these the fault,
  If memory o'er their tomb no trophies raise
Where through the long-drawn aisle and fretted vault
  The pealing anthem swells the note of praise.

Can storied urn or animated bust
  Back to its mansion call the fleeting breath?
Can Honor's voice provoke the silent dust
  Or Flattery soothe the dull cold ear of Death?

Perhaps in this neglected spot is laid
  Some heart once pregnant with celestial fire;
Hands that the rod of empire might have swayed,
  Or wak'd to ecstasy the living lyre;

But Knowledge to their eyes her ample page,
  Rich with the spoils of time, did ne'er unroll;
Chill Penury repressed their noble rage,
  And froze the genial current of the soul.

Full many a gem of purest ray serene.
  The dark, unfathomed caves of ocean bear:
Full many a flower is born to blush unseen,
  And waste its sweetness on the desert air.

Far from the madding crowd's ignoble strife,
  Their sober wishes never learned to stray;
Along the cool sequestered vale of life
  They kept the noiseless tenor of their way.

The Epitaph

Here rests his head upon the lap of earth,
  A youth to fortune and to fame unknown;
Fair Science frown'd not on his humble birth,
  And Melancholy mark'd him for her own.

Large was his bounty, and his soul sincere;
  Heaven did a recompense as largely send:
He gave to misery all he had, a tear;
  He gained from Heaven ('twas all he wished) a friend.

No farther seek his merits to disclose,
  Or draw his frailties from their dread abode, --
(There they alike in trembling hope repose),
  The bosom of his Father and his God.

-- Thomas Gray

A Christian minister once said, "I was never
of any use until I found out that God did not
intend me to be a great man." *--Selected*

A SOLDIER OF THE CROSS

Am I a soldier of the cross,
  A follower of the Lamb?
And shall I fear to own His cause,
  Or blush to speak His name?

Must I be carried to the skies
  On flowery beds of ease,
While others fought to win the prize,
  And sailed through bloody seas?

Are there no foes for me to face?
  Must I not stem the flood?
Is this vile world a friend to grace,
  To help me on to God?

Sure I must fight if I would reign;
  Increase my courage, Lord;
I'll bear the cross, endure the pain,
  Supported by Thy word.

Thy saints, in all this glorious war,
  Shall conquer, though they die;
They view the triumph from afar,
  And seize it with their eye.

When that illustrious day shall rise,
  And all thy armies shine
In robes of victory through the skies,
  The glory shall be Thine.

—Isaac Watts

BUILDING THE BRIDGE FOR HIM

An old man, traveling a lone highway,
Came at evening cold and gray,
　　To a chasm vast and deep and wide,
　　Through which was flowing a sullen tide.
The old man crossed in the twilight dim,
For the sullen stream held no fears for him.
But he turned when he reached the other side,
And built a bridge to span the tide.

"Old man," cried a fellow pilgrim near,
"You are wasting your strength with building here;
Your journey will end with the closing day,
And you never again will pass this way.
"You have crossed the chasm deep and wide.
Why build you a bridge at eventide?"

And the builder lifted his old gray head:
"Good friend, on the path I have come," he said,
"There followeth after me today
A youth whose feet must pass this way.
"This stream, which has been as naught to me,
To that fair-haired boy may a pitfall be;
He, too, must cross in the twilight dim --
Good friend, I am building this bridge for him."

　　　　　　　　-- W. A. Dromgoole

BE STRONG

Be strong!
We are not here to play, to dream, to drift;
We have hard work to do, and loads to lift.
Shun not the struggle; face it.
　'Tis God's gift.

Be strong!
Say not the days are evil--who's to blame?
And fold the hands and acquiesce--O shame!
Stand up, speak out, and bravely,
　In God's name.

Be strong!
It matters not how deep entrenched the wrong,
How hard the battle goes, the day how long,
Faint not, fight on!
　Tomorrow comes the song.

　　　　　　　--Maltbie D. Babcock

Every temptation you overcome makes
you stronger to overcome others; while
every temptation that defeats you makes
you weaker. You can become weaker and
weaker, or you can become stronger and
stronger.　　　　　　　--D. L. Moody

THE CHAMBERED NAUTILUS

This is the ship of pearl which, poets feign,
  Sails the unshadowed main, --
  The venturous bark that flings
On the sweet summer wind its purpled wings
In gulfs enchanted, where the Siren sings,
  And coral reefs lie bare,
Where the cold sea-maids rise to sun their streaming hair.

Its webs of living gauze no more unfurl;
  Wrecked is the ship of pearl!
  And every chambered cell,
Where its dim dreaming life was wont to dwell,
As the frail tenant shaped his growing shell,
  Before thee lies revealed, --
Its irised ceiling rent, its sunless crypt unsealed!

Year after year beheld the silent toil
  That spread his lustrous coil;
  Still, as the spiral grew,
He left the past year's dwelling for the new,
Stole with soft step its shining archway through,
  Built up its idle door,
Stretched in his last-found home, and knew the old no more.

Thanks for the heavenly message brought by thee,
  Child of the wandering sea,
  Cast from her lap, forlorn!
From thy dead lips a clearer note is born

Than ever Triton blew from wreathed horn!
  While on mine ear it rings,
Through the deep caves of thought I hear a voice that sings:--

Build thee more stately mansions, O my soul,
  As the swift seasons roll!
  Leave thy low-vaulted past!
Let each new temple, nobler than the last,
Shut thee from Heaven with a dome more vast,
  Till thou at length art free,
Leaving thine outgrown shell by life's unresting sea!

--Oliver Wendell Holmes

YOUR PLACE

Is your place a small place?
  Tend it with care!--
    He set you there.

Is your place a large place?
  Guard it with care!--
    He set you there.

Whate'er your place, it is
  Not yours alone, but His
    Who set you there.

--John Oxenham

9

THE PRESENT CRISIS
(condensed form)

Once to every man and nation comes the moment to decide;
In the strife of Truth with Falsehood, for the good or evil side;
Some great cause, God's new Messiah, offering each the bloom or blight,
Parts the goats upon the left hand and the sheep upon the right,
And the choice goes by forever 'twixt that darkness and that light.

Hast thou chosen, O my people, on whose party thou shalt stand,
Ere the Doom from its worn sandals shakes the dust against our land?
Though the cause of Evil prosper, yet 'tis Truth alone is strong,
And, albeit she wander outcast now, I see around her throng
Troops of beautiful, tall angels, to enshield her from all wrong.

Careless seems the great Avenger; history's pages but record
One death-grapple in the darkness 'twixt old systems and the Word;
Truth forever on the scaffold, Wrong forever on the throne, --
Yet that scaffold sways the future, and, behind the dim unknown,
Standeth God within the shadow, keeping watch above His own.

Then to side with Truth is noble when we share her wretched crust,
Ere her cause bring fame and profit, and 'tis prosperous to be just;
Then it is the brave man chooses, while the coward stands aside,
Doubting in his abject spirit, till his Lord is crucified,
And the multitude make virtue of the faith they had denied.

Count me o'er the earth's chosen heroes, -- they were souls that stood alone,
While the men they agonized for hurled the contumelious stone,
Stood serene, and down the future saw the golden beam incline
To the side of perfect justice, mastered by their faith divine,
By one man's plain truth to manhood and to God's supreme design.

By the light of burning heretics Christ's bleeding feet I track,
Toiling up new Calvaries ever with the cross that turns not back,
And these mounts of anguish number how each generation learned
One new word of that grand *Credo* which in prophet-hearts hath burned
Since the first man stood God-conquered with his face to heaven upturned.

For humanity sweeps onward: where today the martyr stands,
On the morrow crouches Judas with the silver in his hands;
Far in front the cross stands ready and the crackling fagots burn,
While the hooting mob of yesterday in silent awe return
To glean up the scattered ashes into History's golden urn.

-- James Russell Lowell

NO SCAR?

Hast thou no scar?
No hidden scar on foot, or side, or hand?
I hear thee sung as mighty in the land,
  I hear them hail thy bright ascendant star,
Hast thou no scar?

Hast thou no wound?
Yet I was wounded by the archers, spent,
Leaned me against a tree to die; and rent
  By ravening wolves that compassed me, I swooned;
Hast thou no wound?

No wound? No scar?
Yet, as the Master shall the servant be,
And pierced are the feet that follow Me;
  But thine are whole; can he have followed far
Who hath no wound nor scar?

-- Amy Wilson Carmichael

*"From henceforth let no man trouble me: for I bear in my body the marks
of the Lord Jesus"* (Gal. 6:17).

FREEMEN

Let no man stand between my God and me!
I claim a free man's right
Of intercourse direct with Him,
Who gave me freedom with the air and light.
God made me free--
Let no man stand between
Me and my liberty!

We need no priest to tell us God is love.
Have we not eyes to see,
And minds to apprehend, and hearts
That leap responsive to His charity?
God's gifts are free--
Let no man stand between
Us and His liberty!

We need no priest to point a way to Heaven.
God's heaven is here -- is there --
Man's birthright, with the light and air,
"God is His own and best interpreter."
His ways are free--
Let no man stand between
Us and His liberty!

Let no man strive to rob us of this right!
For this, from age to age,
Our fathers did a mighty warfare wage,
And, by God's help, we'll keep our heritage!

God says--"Be Free!"
And we--
"NO MAN SHALL STAND BETWEEN
OUR SONS AND LIBERTY!"

--John Oxenham

ON HIS BLINDNESS

When I consider how my light is spent,
    Ere half my days, in this dark world and wide,
    And that one talent which is death to hide,
    Lodged with me useless, though my soul more bent
To serve therewith my Maker, and present
    My true account, lest He returning chide,
    'Doth God exact day-labor, light denied,'
    I fondly ask; But patience to prevent
That murmur, soon replies, 'God doth not need
    Either man's work or his own gifts, who best
    Bear His mild yoke, they serve Him best, His state
Is kingly. Thousands at His bidding speed
    And post o'er land and ocean without rest:
    They also serve who only stand and wait.'

--John Milton

Comfort

IN EVERYTHING

In everything? In sorrow, pain, and loss?
   When some hard lesson racks the weary mind?
When, just before, there looms the threat'ning cross?
   When nights are long, and morn brings day unkind?

In everything! Each sorrow and each pain
   Is known by One who measures every day;
And lessons hard, well mastered, will make plain
   The faithful Teacher planning all the way.

Dost know the cross must come before the crown?
   And seed unburied must abide alone?
Dost know the cloud that spreads its sullen frown
   Harms not the sun, whose power must be shown?

Then waiting not for that which shall make clear
   The tender love in what seems harsh and stern,
O Soul redeemed, look up! Dismiss thy fear!
   Now is the time when thanks thou shouldst return!

                -- Author Unknown

No affliction would trouble a child of God, if
he knew God's reasons for sending it. --Morgan

"HE KNOWETH"

("He knoweth them that trust in Him." Nah. 1:7.)

"HE KNOWETH"! Yes -- the dear Lord says He knoweth --
   He knoweth them who trust in Him repose:
Perhaps He wills it should bring saving comfort --
   This blessed fact -- that He His children knows.

"HE KNOWETH," too, what things we here have need of --
   "Your Father knoweth" is the Saviour's word:
And so, whatever things He sees are needful
   Will, in good season, reach us from the Lord.

"HE KNOWETH" also what lies in the darkness;
   So nothing there need make our hearts afraid:
He sees the utmost end from the beginning,--
   And peace is ours as we on Him are stayed.

"HE KNOWETH"! Yes -- of course, He always knoweth --
   And in this blessed fact our hearts may rest,
Rejoicing in the happy calm that cometh
   When we our refuge make within His breast.

                -- J. Danson Smith

SOMETIMES

*"Quenched the violence of fire, escaped the
edge of the sword; ... and others ... were slain
with the sword."*--Heb. 11:34, 35, 37.

Sometimes the lions' mouths are shut;
Sometimes God bids us fight or fly;
Sometimes He feeds us by the brook;
Sometimes the flowing stream runs dry.

Sometimes the burning flames are quenched;
Sometimes with sevenfold heat they glow;
Sometimes His hand divides the waves;
Sometimes His billows overflow.

Sometimes He turns the sword aside;
Sometimes He lets the sharp blade smite;
Sometimes our foes are at our heels,
Sometimes He hides us from their sight.

We may not choose, nor would we dare,
The path in which our feet shall tread;
Enough that He that path hath made,
And He Himself shall walk ahead.

The danger that His love allows
Is safer than our fears may know;
The peril that His care permits
Is our defence where'er we go.

--Annie Johnson Flint

DEARER THAN GOD'S SPARROW

Just think of that odd little sparrow,
    Uncared for by any but God,
It surely must bring thee some comfort
    To know that He loves it--though odd.

That one little odd little sparrow,
    The object of God's tender care?
Then surely thou art of more value,
    Thou need'st not give way to despair.

It may be thou art an " odd sparrow,"
    But God's eye of love rests on thee,
And He understands what to others,
    Will always a mystery be.

Thou thinkest thy case so peculiar
    That nobody can understand,
Take life's tangled skein to Thy Saviour
    And leave it in His skillful Hand.

Believe in His love and His pity
    Confide in His wisdom and care,
Remember the little odd sparrow,
    And never give way to despair.

--Traveling Toward Sunrise

14

ALL'S WELL

Is the pathway dark and dreary?
  God's in His Heaven!
Are you broken, heart-sick, weary?
  God's in His Heaven!
Dreariest roads shall have an ending;
Broken hearts are for God's mending.
    All's well! All's well!
      All's . . . well!

Are life's threads all sorely tangled?
  God's in His Heaven!
Are the sweet chords strained and jangled?
  God's in His Heaven!
Tangled threads are for Love's fingers,
Trembling chords make Heaven's sweet singers.
    All's well! All's well!
      All's . . . well!

Is the burden past your bearing?
  God's in His Heaven!
Hopeless? --Friendless? --No one caring?
  God's in His Heaven!
Burdens shared are light to carry,
Love shall come though long He tarry.
    All's well! All's well!
      All's . . . well!

                    -- John Oxenham
                    in *Bees in Amber*

WITH YOU

Lo, I am with you! With you as I promised!
  What though ye see Me not, nor feel Me near?
Lo, I am with you! rest your heart upon it!
  Lo, I am with you! Always! Now and here!

Lo, I am with you, in the darkest valley!
  Lo, I am with you, in life's brightest hour!
Lo, I am with you, in life's deepest sorrow!
  With you as well in summer's fairest bower!

Lo, I am with you. Now! Henceforth! Forever!
  Ye, who are Mine, by precious blood, My own;
Lo, I am with you --have this for your comfort:
  No hour can be when thou art quite alone.

                    -- J. Danson Smith

O what a happy soul am I
  Although I cannot see,
I am resolved that in this world
  Contented I will be;
How many blessings I enjoy
  That other people don't;
To weep and sigh because I'm blind,
  I cannot and I won't.

                    --Written by Fanny Crosby
                    at the age of eight.

ART THOU WEARY?

Art thou weary, art thou languid,
  Art thou sore distrest?
"Come to Me," saith One, "and coming,
  Be at rest."

Hath He marks to lead me to Him,
  If He be my Guide?
"In His feet and hands are wound prints,
  And His side."

If I still hold closely to Him,
  What hath He at last?
"Sorrow vanquished, labor ended,
  Jordan past."

If I ask Him to receive me,
  Will He say me nay?
"Not till earth and not till Heaven
  Pass away."

--St. Stephen of Mar Saba

THE ZIGZAG PATH

We climbed the height by the zigzag path
  And wondered why--until
We understood it was made zigzag
  To break the force of the hill.

A road straight up would prove too steep
  For the traveler's feet to tread;
The thought was kind in its wise design
  Of a zigzag path instead.

It is so often our daily life;
  We fail to understand
That the twisting way our feet must tread
  By love alone was planned.

Then murmur not at the winding way,
  It is our Father's will
To lead us Home by the zigzag path,
  To break the force of the hill.

--Anonymous

A woman when she was ill, asked whether she wished to live or die, replied, "Which God pleaseth." "But,' said someone standing by, "if God were to refer it to you, which would you choose?" "Truly," said she, "if God were to refer it to me, I would even refer it to Him again."
    --Selected

16

Consecration

OH, TO BE LIKE THEE!

Oh, to be like Thee! blessed Redeemer,
　This is my constant longing and prayer;
Gladly I'll forfeit all of earth's treasures,
　Jesus, Thy perfect likeness to wear.

Oh, to be like Thee! full of compassion,
　Loving, forgiving, tender and kind,
Helping the helpless, cheering the fainting,
　Seeking the wand'ring sinner to find.

Oh, to be like Thee! lowly in spirit,
　Holy and harmless, patient and brave;
Meekly enduring cruel reproaches,
　Willing to suffer others to save.

Oh, to be like Thee! Lord, I am coming,
　Now to receive the anointing divine;
All that I am and have I am bringing,
　Lord, from this moment all shall be Thine.

Oh, to be like Thee! while I am pleading,
　Pour out Thy Spirit, fill with Thy love;
Make me a temple meet for Thy dwelling,
　Fit me for life and Heaven above.

Oh, to be like Thee! oh, to be like Thee,
　Blessed Redeemer, pure as Thou art;
Come in Thy sweetness, come in Thy fullness;
　Stamp Thine own image deep on my heart.

--T. O. Chisholm

　　There is an old story which tells of an Italian duke who went on board a galley ship. As he passed the crew of slaves he asked several of them what their offenses were. Every one laid the blame to someone else, saying his brother was to blame or the judge was bribed. One sturdy young fellow said: "My lord, I am justly in here. I wanted money and I stole it. No one is to blame but myself." The duke on hearing this seized him by the shoulder, saying, "You rogue! What are you doing here among so many honest men? Get you out of their company." The young fellow was then set at liberty, while the rest were left to tug at the oars. 　　　　　　　　　　　　　　　　　　　　　　　--Spurgeon.

DEVOTION

If I had met in Galilee
The Man of sweet humility,
And He had turned and looked on me
   And called me to His side;
What would have been my answ'ring word?
Should I have said, "My Saviour, Lord,
Thou art beyond all else adored,
   Be Thou my Friend and Guide"?

If He had led me, day by day,
In burning heat, 'neath shadows gray,
By dusty path, through tortuous way,
   And asked me to be true;
What would have been my choosing then?
Should I have followed on, e'en when
He took me, from loved home and men,
   To scenes I never knew?

If He had gone before me till
My days were done, and night's cold chill
Had fallen, with its startling thrill,
   Upon my weary soul;
If He had asked me then to lie
In some drear place, 'neath starless sky,
And there, alone, to suffer, die,
   Would He have had control?

Yea, if I'd seen this as my lot,
Knowing my name would be forgot
And my dead body left to rot,
   I should have followed on,
If only, in sweet charity,
My Friend and Guide had stayed with me
And granted me His face to see
   Till life's hard toil had gone:

For love does what the Lover saith,
For love transcends the fear of death,
For love loves on till latest breath,
   And I do love my Friend;--
Then lead me on, my Master-Guide,
Lead where Thou wilt, Thou Crucified,
Since Thou art mine, what'er betide,
   I'll follow to the end!

"Lord, thou knowest all things;
thou knowest that I love thee."

--Henry W. Frost

Some of our hearers do not desire to hear the whole counsel of God. They have their favorite doctrines, and would have us silent on all besides. Many are like the Scotch woman who, after hearing a sermon, said, "It was very well if it hadna been for the trash of duties at the HINNER end."--Spurgeon

HOLD THOU MY HAND

Hold Thou my hand; so weak I am, and helpless,
  I dare not take one step without Thy aid;
Hold Thou my hand; for then, O loving Saviour,
  No dread of ill shall make my soul afraid.

Hold Thou my hand, and closer, closer draw me
  To Thy dear self--my hope, my joy, my all;
Hold Thou my hand, lest haply I should wander,
  And, missing Thee, my trembling feet shall fall.

Hold Thou my hand; the way is dark before me
  Without the sunlight of Thy face divine;
But when by faith I catch its radiant glory,
  What heights of joy, what rapturous songs are mine!

Hold Thou my hand, that when I reach the margin
  Of that lone river Thou didst cross for me,
A heavenly light may flash along its waters,
  And ev'ry wave like crystal bright shall be.

                    --Fanny J. Crosby

WHICH?

Which shall I choose today,
  The hard or easy way;
To seek some soul to bless,
  Or stay in idleness;
For some cause to sacrifice
  Or simply close my eyes;
Work out God's plan for me,
  Or set my passions free;
Climb upward on my knees,
  Or only seek for ease;
Walk where the martyrs trod,
  Or scorn the claims of God?

Lord, in my heart today,
  I give Thee right of way,
Work both to will and do
  And help me to be true.

                    --Author Unknown

Difficulties are God's errands; and when we
are sent upon them, we should esteem it a
proof of God's confidence.   --Beecher

19

GOD'S WAY

Thy way, not mine, O Lord!
  However dark it be;
Lead me by Thine own hand,
  Choose out the path for me.

Smooth let it be, or rough,
  It will be still the best;
Winding or straight, it matters not,
  It leads me to Thy rest.

I dare not choose my lot,
  I would not, if I might;
Choose Thou for me, O God!
  So shall I walk aright.

The kingdom that I seek
  Is Thine; so let the way
That leads to it be Thine;
  Else I must surely stray.

Take Thou my cup, and it
  With joy or sorrow fill,
As best to Thee may seem;
  Choose Thou my good or ill.

Not mine, not mine the choice
  In things of great or small;
Be Thou my guide, my strength,
  My wisdom and my all.

--Horatius Bonar
1808-1889

I SOUGHT THE LORD

"I sought the Lord, and afterward I knew
He moved my soul to seek Him, seeking me;
It was not I that found, O Saviour true,
No, I was found of Thee.

"Thou didst reach forth Thine hand and mine enfold;
I walked and sank not on the storm-vexed sea--
'Twas not so much that I on Thee took hold,
As Thou, dear Lord, on me.

"I find, I walk, I love, but oh, the whole
Of love is but my answer, Lord, to Thee;
For Thou wast long beforehand with my soul,
Always Thou lovedst me."

--Selected

Bigness in God's sight is measured in terms of quality,
not quantity.
    --Bob Jones, Jr.

THE INN OF LIFE

As It was in the Beginning, --
Is Now, --
And . . . . ?

ANNO DOMINI I

"No room!
No room!
The Inn is full,
Yea -- overfull.
No room have we
For such as ye --
Poor folk of Galilee,
    Pass on! Pass on!"

"Nay then! --
Your charity
Will ne'er deny
Some corner mean,
Where she may lie unseen.
For see! --
Her time is nigh."

"Alack! And she
So young and fair!
Place have we none;
And yet -- how bid ye gone?
Stay then! -- out there
Among the beasts
Ye may find room,
And eke a truss
To lie upon."

ANNO DOMINI 1913, etc., etc.

"No room!
No room!
No room for Thee,
Thou Man of Galilee!
The house is full,
Yea, overfull.
There is no room for Thee, --
    Pass on! Pass on!

"Nay -- see!
The place is packed.
We scarce have room
For our own selves,

So how shall we
Find room for Thee,
Thou Man of Galilee, --
    Pass on! Pass on!

"But -- if Thou shouldst
This way again,
And we can find
So much as one small corner
Free from guest,
Not then in vain
Thy quest.
But now --
The house is full.
    Pass on!"

Christ passes
On His ceaseless quest,
Nor will He rest
With any,
Save as Chiefest Guest.

                            -- John Oxenham

Mr. Spurgeon tells a story of a man who used to say to his wife: "Mary, go to church and pray for us both." But the man dreamed one night, when he and his wife got to the gate of Heaven, Peter said: *"Mary, go in for both."* He awoke and made up his mind that it was time for him to become a Christian on his own account.

Courage

THE PATH OF LIFE

Dear Master, the way has *darkened;*
  I cannot see now ahead;
Nor shines there a light to guide me,
  No light--but Thyself instead.

The way, too, grows strangely *narrow,*
  No longer 'tis gay and free;
But narrow, yes, oh, so narrow,
  Just room for Thyself and me!

The path has grown quickly *lonely,*
  Earth's voices I no more hear;
But Thou, precious Lord, art with me,
  And where is my cause for fear?

Where leads such unwelcome pathway--
  Unwelcome--to human view;
Both darksome, narrow and lonely,
  Path trodden by, oh, so few?

It leads to the place of dying,
  To die, that He more may live:
It leads to the place of losing,
  That He may His fulness give.

And so, though the path be darkened,
  And narrow and lonely, too,
And if, yes, if self is buried
  Far down, down, down out of view;

What then? Ah, unending glory!
  The sure "path of life" 'twill be:
Of life, endless life and blessing,
  Lived out by Himself in me.

Lead on, blessed Lord, I follow--
  To this "path of life" oh, lead;
And when, at its end, I meet Thee,
  My Heaven will be Heaven indeed.

--J. Danson Smith

I'M STANDING, LORD

"I'm standing, Lord.
There is a mist that blinds my sight.
Steep jagged rocks, front, left, and right,
Lower, dim, gigantic, in the night.
  Where is the way?

"I'm standing, Lord.
The black rock hems me in behind.
Above my head a moaning wind
Chills and oppresses heart and mind.
  I am afraid!

"I'm standing, Lord.
The rock is hard beneath my feet.
I nearly slipped, Lord, on the sleet.
So weary, Lord, and where a seat?
  Still must I stand?"

He answered me, and on His face
A look ineffable of grace,
Of perfect, understanding love,
Which all my murmuring did remove.

"I'm standing, Lord.
Since Thou hast spoken, Lord, I see
Thou hast beset; these rocks are Thee;
And since Thy love encloses me,
  I stand and sing!"

--Betty Stam, Martyred in China

PROMISED STRENGTH

One day when my burden seemed greater
  Than my body and spirit could bear,
Weighed down by the load, I faltered
  Beneath my sorrow and care;
And I cried to the heedless silence
  As I walked where I could not see:
"Where is the strength that is promised?
  Where is the strength for me?"

And suddenly out of the stillness,
  A voice came clear and true:
"My child, you are striving to carry
  A burden not meant for you,
And the thought of the years outstretching
  Before you has darkened the way,
While the only strength I have promised
  Is the sure strength day by day."

I took one step--and I found it
  Quite easy, indeed, to take,
And the burden slid from my shoulders
  And my heart that was ready to break
Gave thanks that my eyes were opened
  And my shoulders were eased of their load,
As I saw, step by step I was strengthened
  To walk on the roughest road!

--Grace Noll Crowell

Honey is dear bought if licked from thorns. --Anonymous

23

I TAKE, HE UNDERTAKES

I take salvation full and free,
Through Him who gave His life for me,
He undertakes my all to be--
   "I take"--"He undertakes."

I take Him as my holiness,
My spirit's spotless, heavenly dress,
I take the Lord my righteousness,
   "I take"--"He undertakes."

I take the promised Holy Ghost,
I take the power of Pentecost,

To fill me to the uttermost.
   "I take"--"He undertakes."

I simply take Him at His word,
I praise Him that my prayer is heard,
And claim my answer from the Lord.
   "I take"--"He undertakes."

"I take Thee, blessed Lord,
   I give myself to Thee;
And Thou, according to Thy Word,
   Dost undertake for me."

--Rev. A. B. Simpson.

A PRAYER FOR COURAGE

This, too, will pass. O heart, say it over and over,
Out of your deepest sorrow, out of your deepest grief,
No hurt can last forever -- perhaps tomorrow
Will bring relief.

This, too, will pass. It will spend itself -- its fury
Will die as the wind dies down with the setting sun;
Assuaged and calm, you will rest again, forgetting
A thing that is done.

Repeat it again and again, O heart, for your comfort;
This, too, will pass as surely as passed before
The old forgotten pain, and the other sorrows
That once you bore.

As certain as stars at night, or dawn after darkness,
Inherent as the lift of the blowing grass,
Whatever your despair or your frustration --
This, too, will pass.

--Grace Noll Crowell

Death and Heaven

THEY COME!

From North and South, and East and West,
    They come!
The sorely tried, the much oppressed,
Their Faith and Love to manifest,
    They come!
They come to tell of work well done,
They come to tell of kingdoms won,
To worship at the Great White Throne,
    They come!
In a noble consecration,
With a sound of jubilation,
    They come! They come!

Through tribulations and distress,
    They come!
Through perils great and bitterness,
Through persecutions pitiless,
    They come!
They come by paths the martyrs trod,

They come from underneath the rod,
Climbing through darkness up to God,
    They come!
Out of mighty tribulation,
With a sound of jubilation,
    They come! They come!

From every land beneath the sun,
    They come!
To tell of mighty victories won;
Unto the Father through the Son,
    They come!
They come -- the victors in the fight,
They come -- the blind restored to sight,
From deepest Darkness into Light;
    They come!
In a holy exaltation,
With a sound of jubilation,
    They come! They come!

-- John Oxenham

25

LIFE THROUGH DEATH

There is no gain but by a loss,
You cannot save but by a cross,
The corn of wheat to multiply
Must fall into the ground and die.

Wherever you ripe fields behold,
Waving to God their sheaves of gold,
Be sure some corn of wheat has died,
Some soul has there been crucified;
Someone has wrestled, wept, and prayed,
And fought hell's legions undismayed.

Life everywhere replaces death,
In earth and sea and sky;
And that the rose may breathe its breath,
Some living thing must die.

But all through life I see a cross
Where sons of God yield up their breath;
There is no gain except by loss,
There is no life except by death,
And no full vision except by faith,
Nor glory but by wearing shame,
Nor justice but by taking blame,
And that Eternal Passion saith,
"Be emptied of glory and right and name."

--Selected

THE SANDS OF TIME

The sands of time are sinking,
  The dawn of Heaven breaks,
The summer morn I've sighed for,
  The fair, sweet morn awakes.
Dark, dark hath been the midnight,
  But dayspring is at hand,
And 'glory, glory dwelleth
  In Immanuel's land.

--Anne Ross Cousin

THE BEYOND

It seemeth such a little way to me
Across to that strange country, the Beyond;
And yet not strange, for it has grown to be
The home of those of whom I am most fond;
And so to me there is no sting to Death.
It is but crossing, with suspended breath
And white, set face, a little strip of sea,
To find the loved ones on the other shore
More beautiful, more precious than before.
——Ella Wheeler Wilcox

OUR BABY

Today we cut the fragrant sod,
  With trembling hands, asunder,
And lay this well-beloved of God,
  Our dear, dead baby under.
O hearts that ache, and ache afresh!
  O tears too blindly raining!
Our hearts are weak, yet, being flesh,
  Too strong for our restraining!

Sleep, darling, sleep! Cold rain shall steep
  Thy little turf-made dwelling;
Thou wilt not know, so far below,
  What winds or storms are swelling;
And birds shall sing in the warm spring,
  And flowers bloom about thee:
Thou wilt not heed them, love; but oh,
  The loneliness without thee!

Father, we will be comforted!
  Thou wast the gracious Giver;
We yield her up, not dead, not dead,
  To dwell with Thee forever!
Take Thou our child, ours for a day,
  Thine while the ages blossom!
This little shining head we lay
  In the Redeemer's bosom!

-- Author Unknown

HE'S HOME AT LAST!

Safe Home at last! Oh say not he has died.
His soul has only crossed the swelling tide,
And Heaven's gates for him have opened wide--
    He's Home at last!

A true and valiant warrior of the Faith,
Proclaiming Christ e'en with his latest breath,
Has laid his armor down--call it not death.
    He's Home at last!

He now beholds, with eyes undimmed by tears,
The face of Him who through the passing years,
Has been his stay, dispelling doubt and fears.
    He's Home at last!

And though his going leaves a void within
Our lonely hearts, we can rejoice with him,
His race is run, Heav'n's glory he hath seen.
    He's Home at last!

At Home, with those on earth he loved so well,
Who now within the walls of jasper dwell,
Oh bliss beyond all mortal pow'r to tell!
    He's Home at last!

Life's sun for him has set--but oh the glow
That long will linger o'er this world of woe,
Because he lived and labored here below!
    He's Home at last!

--Avis B. Christiansen

THE HOLY CITY

Last night I lay a-sleeping,
There came a dream so fair;
I stood in old Jerusalem,
Beside the Temple there;
I heard the children singing,
And ever as they sang,
Methought the voice of angels
From Heaven in answer rang,
  Jerusalem, Jerusalem,
  Lift up your gates and sing
  Hosanna in the highest,
  Hosanna to your King!

And then methought my dream was changed,
The streets no longer rang;
Hushed were the glad Hosannas
The little children sang;
The sun grew dark with mystery,
The morn was cold and chill,
As the shadow of a cross arose
Upon a lonely hill.
  Jerusalem, Jerusalem,
  Hark! how the angels sing,
  Hosanna in the highest,
  Hosanna to your King!

And once again the scene was changed,
New earth there seemed to be!
I saw the holy city
Beside the tideless sea;
The light of God was on its street,
The gates were open wide;
And all who would might enter,
And no one was denied.

No need of moon or stars by night,
Nor sun to shine by day;
It was the New Jerusalem,
That would not pass away.
  Jerusalem, Jerusalem,
  Sing, for the night is o'er,
  Hosanna in the highest,
  Hosanna for evermore!

--F. E. Weatherly

A mother asked her six-year-old what loving-kindness meant. "Well," he said, "when I ask you for a piece of bread and butter and you give it to me, that's kindness, but WHEN YOU PUT JAM ON IT, THAT'S LOVING-KINDNESS."
--Chicago Tribune

A DEATH BED

As I lay sick upon my bed
  I heard them say "in danger."
The word seemed very strange to me;
  Could any word seem stranger?

"In danger" of escape from sin,
  Forever and forever?
Of entering that most holy place
  Where evil enterest never?

"In danger" of beholding Him,
  Who is my soul's salvation,
Whose promises sustain my soul
  In blest anticipation?

"In danger" of soon shaking off
  Earth's last remaining fetter,
And of departing hence to be
  With Christ which is far better?

It is a solemn thing to die,
  To face the King Immortal;
And each forgiven sinner should
  Tread softly o'er the portal.

But when we have confessed our sins
  To Him who can discern them,
And God has given pardon, peace,
  Tho' we could ne'er deserve them,

Then dying is no dangerous thing;
  Safe in the Saviour's keeping,
The ransomed one is gently led
  Beyond the reach of weeping.

--Martha Snell Nicholson

STEPPING ASHORE

Oh, think to step ashore,
  And find it Heaven;
To clasp a hand outstretched,
  And find it God's hand!
To breathe new air,
  And that, celestial air;
To feel refreshed,
  And find it immortality;
Ah, think to step from storm and stress
  To one unbroken calm:
To awake and find it Home.

--Robert E. Selle

Little faith will bring your soul
to Heaven; great faith will bring
Heaven to your soul.   --Spurgeon

NIGHTFALL

Fold up the tent!
The sun is in the west.
Tomorrow my untented soul will range
Among the blest,
  And I am well content,
  For what is sent, is sent,
  And God knows best.

Fold up the tent,
And speed the parting guest!
The night draws on, though night and day are one
On this long quest.
  This house was only lent
  For my apprenticement--
  What is, is best.

Fold up the tent!
Its slack ropes all undone,
Its pole all broken, and its cover rent--
Its work is done.
  But mine--tho' spoiled and spent
  Mine earthly tenement--
  Is but begun.

Fold up the tent!
Its tenant would be gone,
To fairer skies than mortal eyes
May look upon.

All that I loved has passed,
And left me at the last
Alone!--alone!

Fold up the tent!
Above the mountain's crest,
I hear a clear voice calling, calling clear,
"To rest! To rest!"
  And I am glad to go,
  For the sweet oil is low,
  And rest is best!

--John Oxenham

CONVINCED BY SORROW

"There is no God," the foolish saith,
  But none, "There is no sorrow."
And nature oft the cry of faith,
  In bitter need will borrow;
Eyes which the preacher could not school,
  By wayside graves are raised,
And lips say "God be pitiful,"
  Who ne'er said, "God be praised."
    Be pitiful, O God !

--Elizabeth Barrett Browning

THIS ISN'T DEATH

This isn't death, it's glory;
It isn't dark, it's light;
It isn't stumbling, groping,
Or even faith--it's sight.

This isn't grief, it's having
My last tear wiped away;
It's sunrise--the morning
Of my eternal day.

This isn't even praying;
It's speaking face to face.
It's listening and it's glimpsing
The wonders of His grace.

This is the end of all pleading
For strength to bear my pain;
Not even pain's dark memory
Will ever live again.

How did I bear the earth life
Before I came up higher,
Before my soul was granted
Its every deep desire?

Before I knew this rapture
Of meeting face to face
That ONE who sought me, saved me,
And kept me by His grace?

--Martha Snell Nicholson

HOMING

From sweetest songs of earth, from love and laughter,
From jewelled joys, when glory dies in gloaming,
Turn I to Thee, as swallow to her rafter,
Glad with Thy world, but homing.

From piercing pain, from earth's relentless sorrow,
As frightened bird, and wounded in its roaming,
Haste I to Thee, Thy quietness to borrow,
Broken, forspent--but homing.

Straight to Thy heart, O Love that changest never,
Glad with Thy world, or wounded in its roaming,
Shining and swift, or broken-winged, but ever
Homing.

--E. Margaret Clarkson

THE CLEARER VISION

When, with bowed head,
And silent-streaming tears,
With mingled hopes and fears,
To earth we yield our dead;
The saints, with clearer sight,
Do cry in glad accord,
"A soul released from prison
Is risen, is risen --
Is risen to the glory of the Lord."

--John Oxenham

31

Decision

CHOOSE FOR THYSELF

Go with the tide, young man, go with the tide;
Thousands will grip your hand, walk by your side,
  Smile at the wrongs that crush,
  Wink at the lies, nor blush
  When in the slime and slush
Virtue her face shall hide.

Stand ever right, young man, stand ever right;
Lonely you'll be and sad in such a fight;
  Strike for the good and true,
  March with the unbought few,
  Clouds will hang over you
With not a star in sight.

Ah, but 'twere best, young man, forever best,
Best to go down alone in such a quest;
  Best to be cursed, and lie
  Bleeding while foes march by
  Than that thy soul should die,
Treason-stained and distressed!

-- Robert P. (Bob) Shuler

THE WAYS

To every man there openeth
A way, and ways, and a way.
And the high soul climbs the high way,
And the low soul gropes the low,
And in between, on the misty flats,
The rest drift to and fro.
But to every man there openeth
A high way, and a low.
And every man decideth
The way his soul shall go.

-- John Oxenham

One may be better than his repu-
tation, but never better than his
principles.
-Anonymous

32

GADARA, A. D. 31

Rabbi, begone! Thy powers
Bring loss to us and ours.
Our ways are not as Thine.
Thou lovest men, we -- swine.
Oh, get you hence, Omnipotence,
And take this fool of Thine!
His soul? What care we for his soul?
What good to us that Thou hast made him whole,
Since we have lost our swine?

And Christ went sadly.
He had wrought for them a sign
Of Love, and Hope, and Tenderness divine;
They wanted -- swine.
Christ stands without *your* door and gently knocks;
But if your gold, or swine, the entrance blocks,
He forces no man's hold -- He will depart,
And leave you to the treasures of your heart.

No cumbered chamber will the Master share,
But one swept bare
By cleansing fires, then plenished fresh and fair
With meekness, and humility, and prayer.
There will He come, yet, coming, even there
He stands and waits, and will no entrance win
Until the latch be lifted from within.

-- John Oxenham

THE NAMELESS SEEKER

We are not told his name -- this "rich young ruler"
  Who sought the Lord that day;
We only know that he had great possession
  And that -- he went away.

He went away -- from joy and peace and power;
  From love unguessed, untold;
From that eternal life that he was seeking,
  Back to his paltry gold.

He went away; he kept his earthly treasure,
  But oh, at what a cost!
Afraid to take the cross and lose his riches --
  And God and Heaven were lost.

So for the tinsel bonds that held and drew him
  What honor he let slip --
Comrade of John and Paul and friend of Jesus --
  What glorious fellowship!

For they who left their all to follow Jesus
  Have found a deathless fame,
On His immortal scroll of saints and martyrs
  God wrote each shining name.

We should have read his there -- the rich young ruler --
  If he had stayed that day;
Nameless -- though Jesus loved him -- ever nameless
  Because -- he went away.

-- Author Unknown

Home

HOME

It takes a heap o' livin' in a house t' make it home,
A heap o' sun an' shadder, an' ye sometimes have t' roam
Afore ye really 'preciate the things ye lef' behind,
An' hunger fer 'em somehow, with 'em allus on yer mind.
It don't make any differunce how rich ye get t' be,
How much yer chairs an' tables cost, how great yer luxury;
It ain't home t' ye, though it be the palace of a king,
Until somehow yer soul is sort o' wrapped 'round everything.

Home ain't a place that gold can buy or get up in a minute;
Afore it's home there's got t' be a heap o' livin' in it;
Within the walls there's got t' be some babies born, and then
Right there ye've got t' bring 'em up t' women good, an' men;
And gradjerly, as time goes on, ye find ye wouldn't part
With anything they ever used--they've grown into yer heart:
The old high chairs, the playthings, too, the little shoes they wore
Ye hoard; an' if ye could ye'd keep the thumbmarks on the door.

Ye've got t' weep t' make it home, ye've got t' sit an' sigh
An' watch beside a loved one's bed, an' know that Death is nigh;
An' in the stillness o' the night t' see Death's angel come,
An' close the eyes o' her that smiled, an' leave her sweet voice dumb.
Fer these are scenes that grip the heart, an' when yer tears are dried,
Ye find the home is dearer than it was, an' sanctified;
An' tuggin' at ye always are the pleasant memories
O' her that was an' is no more--ye can't escape from these.

Ye've got t' sing an' dance fer years, ye've got t' romp an' play,
An' learn t' love the things ye have by usin' 'em each day;
Even the roses 'round the porch must blossom year by year
Afore they 'come a part o' ye, suggestin' someone dear
Who used t' love 'em long ago, an' trained 'em jes' t' run
The way they do, so's they would get the early mornin' sun;
Ye've got t' love each brick an' stone from cellar up t' dome:
It takes a heap o' livin' in a house t' make it home.

--Edgar A. Guest

MOTHER'S WORK

Nobody knows of the work it makes,
  To keep the home together;
Nobody knows of the steps it takes,
  Nobody knows--but Mother.

Nobody listens to childish woes,
  Which kisses only smother;
Nobody's pained by the naughty blows,
  Nobody--only Mother.

Nobody knows of the sleepless care
  Bestowed on baby brother;
Nobody knows of the tender prayer,
  Nobody knows--but Mother.

Nobody knows of the lessons taught
  Of loving one another;
Nobody knows of the patience sought,
  Nobody--only Mother.

Nobody knows of anxious fears
  Lest darlings may not weather

The storms of life in after years,
  Nobody knows--but Mother.

Nobody knows of the tears that start,
  The grief she'd gladly smother,
Nobody knows of the breaking heart,
  Nobody--only Mother.

Nobody clings to the wayward child,
  Though scorned by every other,
Leads it so gently from pathways wild,
  Nobody can--but Mother.

Nobody knows of the hourly prayer,
  For him, our erring brother,
Pride of her heart, once so pure and fair,
  Nobody--only Mother.

Nobody kneels at the throne above
  To thank the Heavenly Father
For that sweetest gift—a mother's love.
  Nobody can--but Mother.

-- Flora Hamilton Cassel

SEND THEM TO BED WITH A KISS

O mothers, so weary, discouraged,
  Worn out with the cares of the day,
You often grow cross and impatient,
  Complain of the noise and the play;
For the day brings so many vexations,
  So many things going amiss;
But, mothers, whatever may vex you,
  Send the children to bed with a kiss!

The dear little feet wander often,
  Perhaps, from the pathway of right,
The dear little hands find new mischief
  To try you from morning till night;
But think of the desolate mothers
  Who'd give all the world for your bliss,
And, as thanks for your infinite blessings,
  Send the children to bed with a kiss!

For some day their noise will not vex you,
  The silence will hurt you far more;
You will long for their sweet childish voices,
  For a sweet childish face at the door;
And to press a child's face to your bosom,
  You'd give all the world for just this!
For the comfort 'twill bring you in sorrow,
  Send the children to bed with a kiss!

-- From " New Orleans Picayune"

THE WATCHER

She always leaned to watch for us,
  Anxious if we are late--
In winter by the window,
  In summer by the gate.

And though we mocked her tenderly,
  Who had such foolish care,
The long way home would seem more safe
  Because she waited there.

Her thoughts were all so full of us,
  She never could forget!
And so I think that where she is
  She must be watching yet.

Waiting till we come home to her,
  Anxious if we were late,
Watching from Heaven's window--
  Leaning from Heaven's gate.

--Margaret Widdemer

A little boy entered a shop, in the window of which was a card, "Boy Wanted." Thinking he was too weak for the work, the gentleman said, " Well, my lad, what can you do?" The boy replied, "I can do what I'm told, sir." This so pleased the shopkeeper that he said, "You'll do, my boy."

BEAUTIFUL HANDS

Such beautiful, beautiful hands,
  They're neither white nor small,
And you, I know, would scarcely think
  That they were fair at all.
I've looked on hands whose form and hue
  A sculptor's dream might be,
Yet are these aged wrinkled hands
  Most beautiful to me.

Such beautiful, beautiful hands!
  Though heart were weary and sad
These patient hands kept toiling on
  That the children might be glad.
I almost weep when looking back
  To childhood's distant day!
I think how these hands rested not
  When mine were at their play.

But, oh! beyond this shadow land,
  Where all is bright and fair;
I know full well these dear old hands
  Will palms of victory bear;
Where crystal streams, through endless years
Flow over golden sands,
And where the old are young again,
I'll clasp my mother's hands.

-- Ellen M. H. Gates

"THE LORD GIVETH"

  God lent him to me for my very own,
Let me become his father, me alone!
Gave him to me not for an hour--for years!
('Tis gratefulness gleams in my eyes, not tears.)
No joy that fathers know but it was mine
In fathering that laddie strong and fine.

Time after time I said: " 'Tis but a dream;
I shall awake to find things only seem
Grand as they are." Yet still he lingered on
Till year on sweeter year had come and gone.
My heart is filled forever with a song
Because God let me have my lad so long.

He was my own until I fully knew
And never could forget how deep and true
A father's love for his own son may be.
It drew me nearer God Himself; for He
Has loved His Son. (These are but grateful tears
That he was with me all those happy years!)

--Strickland Gillilan

If we had paid no more attention to our
plants than we have to our children, we
would now be living in a jungle of weeds.
--Burbank

Jesus

SCARRED

The shame He suffered left its brand
In gaping wound in either hand;
Sin's penalty He deigned to meet
Has torn and scarred His blessed feet;
The condemnation by Him borne
Marred His brow with print of thorn.
Trespass and guilt for which He died
Have marked Him with a riven side.

Mine was the shame, the penalty;
The sin was mine; it was for me
He felt the nails, the thorns, the spear.
For love of me the scars appear
In hands and feet and side and brow.
Beholding them I can but bow
Myself a living sacrifice
To Him who paid so dear a price.

--Bob Jones, Jr.

FOREVER NEAR

There is an eye that never sleeps
  Beneath the wing of night;
There is an ear that never shuts
  When sink the beams of light.

There is an arm that never tires
  When human strength gives way;
There is a love that never fails
  When earthly loves decay.

That eye is fixed on seraph throngs;
  That arm upholds the sky;
That ear is filled with angel songs;
  That love is throned on high.

But there's a power which man can wield,
  When mortal aid is vain,
That eye, that arm, that love to reach,
  That listening ear to gain.

That power is prayer, which soars on high,
  Through Jesus, to the throne,
And moves the hand which moves the world,
  To bring salvation down.

--John A. Wallace

38

YEARNING FOR JESUS

Jesus, thou Joy of loving hearts!
  Thou Fount of life! Thou Light of men!
From the best bliss that earth imparts
  We turn unfilled to Thee again.

Thy truth unchanged hath ever stood;
  Thou savest those that on Thee call;
To them that seek Thee, Thou art good,
  To them that find Thee, all in all.

We taste Thee, O Thou living Bread!
  And long to feast upon Thee still;
We drink of Thee, the Fountain Head,
  And thirst from Thee our souls to fill.

Our restless spirits yearn for Thee,
  Where'er our changeful lot is cast;
Glad, when Thy gracious smile we see,
  Blest, when our faith can hold Thee fast.

O Jesus, ever with us stay!
  Make all our moments calm and bright!
Chase the dark night of sin away!
  Shed o'er the world Thy holy light!

--Bernard of Clairvaux,
Translated by Ray Palmer

WHAT CHRIST IS TO US

The Shield from every dart;
The Balm for every smart;
The Sharer of each load;
Companion on the road.

The Door into the fold;
The Anchor that will hold;
The Shepherd of the sheep;
The Guardian of my sleep.

The Friend with Whom I talk;
The Way by which I walk;
The Light to show the way;
The Strength for every day.

The Source of my delight;
The Song to cheer the night;
The Thought that fills my mind;
The Best of All to find--is Jesus!

--Anonymous

HE DIED--BUT LIVES!

I hear the words of love,
  I gaze upon the blood;
I see the mighty sacrifice,
  And I have peace with God.
'Tis everlasting peace,
  Sure as Jehovah's name;
'Tis stable as His steadfast throne,
  For evermore the same.

The clouds may go and come,
  And storms may sweep my sky;
This blood-sealed friendship changes not,
  The cross is ever nigh.
My love is ofttimes low,
  My joy still ebbs and flows;
But peace with Him remains the same.
  No change Jehovah knows.

That which can shake the cross
  May shake the peace it gave,
Which tells me Christ has never died,
  Or never left the grave.
Till then my peace is sure,
  It will not, cannot yield;
Jesus, I know, has died and lives;
  On this firm rock I build.

I change, He changes not,
  The Christ can never die;
His love, not mine, the resting place,
  His truth, not mine, the tie.
The cross still stands unchanged,
  Though Heaven is now His home;
The mighty stone is rolled away,
  But yonder is His tomb.

And yonder is my peace,
  The grave of all my woes;
I know the Son of God has come,
  I know He died and rose.
I know He liveth now
  At God's right hand above;
I know the throne on which He sits,
  I know His truth and love.

--Horatius Bonar

MY ADVOCATE

I sinned. And straightway, posthaste, Satan flew
Before the presence of the most High God,
And made a railing accusation there.
He said, "This soul, this thing of clay and sod,
Has sinned. 'Tis true that he has named Thy Name,
But I demand his death, for Thou hast said,
'The soul that sinneth, it shall die.' Shall not
Thy sentence be fulfilled? Is justice dead?
Send now this wretched sinner to his doom.
What other thing can righteous ruler do?"
And thus he did accuse me day and night,
And every word he spoke, O God, was true!

Then quickly One rose from God's right hand,
Before whose glory angels veiled their eyes;
He spoke, "Each jot and tittle of the law
Must be fulfilled; the guilty sinner dies!
But wait--suppose his guilt were all transferred
To Me, and that I paid his penalty!
Behold My hands, My side, My feet! One day
I was made sin for him, and died that he
Might be presented faultless, at Thy throne!"
And Satan fled away. Full well he knew
That he could not prevail against such love,
For every word my dear Lord spoke was true!

--Martha Snell Nicholson

SUPPOSE!

Suppose that Christ had not been born
That far away Judean morn.
Suppose that God, whose mighty hand
Created worlds, had never planned
A way for man to be redeemed.
Suppose the wise men only dreamed
That guiding star whose light still glows
Down through the centuries. Suppose
Christ never walked here in men's sight,
Our blessed Way, and Truth, and Light.

Suppose He counted all the cost,
And never cared that we were lost,
And never died for you and me,
Nor shed His blood on Calvary
Upon the shameful cross. Suppose
That having died, He never rose,
And there was none with power to save
Our souls from death beyond the grave!
O far away Judean morn,
Suppose that Christ had not been born!

--Martha Snell Nicholson

41

ON THE EMMAUS ROAD

It happened on a solemn eventide,
Soon after He that was our Surety died,
Two bosom friends, each pensively inclined,
The scene of all those sorrows left behind,
Sought their own village, busy as they went
In musings worthy of the great event:

They spake of Him they loved, of Him whose life,
Though blameless, had incurred perpetual strife,
Whose deeds had left, in spite of hostile arts,
A deep memorial graven on their hearts.
The recollection, like a vein of ore,
The farther traced, enriched them still the more;
They thought Him, and they justly thought Him, one
Sent to do more than He appeared to have done:
To exalt a people, and to place them high
Above all else, and wondered He should die.

Ere yet they brought their journey to an end,
A Stranger joined them, courteous as a friend,
And asked them, with a kind, engaging air
What their affliction was, and begged a share.
Informed, He gathered up the broken thread
And, truth and wisdom gracing all He said,
Explained, illustrated, and searched so well
The tender theme on which they chose to dwell,
That, reaching home, "The night," they said, "is near,
We must not now be parted, sojourn here."

The new Acquaintance soon became a guest,
And, made so welcome at their simple feast,
He blessed the bread, but vanished at the word,
And left them both exclaiming, "It was the LORD!
Did not our hearts feel all He deigned to say?
Did they not burn within us by the way?"

--William Cowper

NEW CALVARY

So one by one they turned away from Him,
Until He stood alone on Pilate's floor;
A tired young Man, yet stalwart, straight, and slim,
Whose heart was broken, yet whose visage bore
Such depths of peace the rulers paused, afraid,
And murmured, "Tell the sin this Man has done."
(In all Jerusalem none came to aid.)
The cry rang back, "He says He is God's Son!"

He says He is God's Son. . .Oh, where were they,
The halt, the deaf, the blind He had made well?
Why did they not come running swift to say,
"We are His proof!" They had so much to tell!
I censure them—and yet because of me
Christ kneels alone sometimes in Calvary.

--Helen Welshimer

WAS JESUS GOD?

Was Jesus God, the Babe of Bethlehem,
    Who took upon Himself the form of man;
Was He in very deed the great I Am,
    Who came to carry out the Father's Plan?

Was Jesus God, the Boy of Nazareth,
    Who listened to the temple priests of old;
Was He the great Creator of the world,
    The One who wooed and won me to His fold?

Was Jesus God, the Man of Galilee,
    Who taught and worked His miracles divine;
And does He sit upon the throne of God,
    The One who dwells within this heart of mine?

Was Jesus God, and will He be my judge,
    When in the clouds He comes to earth again;
Is He the One to whom all knees must bow,
    The Christ who some day o'er the world will reign?

Yes, He was God, and He is God today,
    No other could have paid the price of sin;
'Twas God who trod earth's roads so long ago
    And yet He deigns to dwell my heart within.

                              --Oswald J. Smith

WHITHER GAZING?

Too often we sigh and look WITHIN;
    Jesus sighed and looked WITHOUT.

We sigh and look DOWN;
    Jesus sighed and looked UP.

We sigh and look to EARTH;
    Jesus sighed and looked to
        HEAVEN.

We sigh and look to MAN;
    Jesus sighed and looked to
        GOD.

                    --Selected

THE OMNIPOTENT

O God, who cradles the moon in thine arm
    And hangs the stars in place,
Mighty Creator of the universe,
    God of time and space--
Before the beginning of time Thou wert there
    And after it ends Thou wilt be.
From everlasting to everlasting Thou art,
    And still Thou art mindful of me!

                    --Margaret Wendel

IF JESUS CAME TO YOUR HOUSE

If Jesus came to your house to spend a day or two--
If He came unexpectedly, I wonder what you'd do.
Oh, I know you'd give your nicest room to such an honored Guest,
And all the food you'd serve to Him would be the very best,
And you would keep assuring Him you're glad to have Him there--
That serving Him in your home is joy beyond compare.

But--when you saw Him coming, would you meet Him at the door
With arms outstretched in welcome to your heav'nly Visitor?
Or would you have to change your clothes before you let Him in? Or hide
Some magazines and put the Bible where they'd been?
Would you turn off the radio and hope He hadn't heard?
And wish you hadn't uttered that last, loud, hasty word?

Would you hide your worldly music and put some hymn books out?
Could you let Jesus walk right in, or would you rush about?
And I wonder--if the Savior spent a day or two with you,
Would you go right on doing the things you always do?
Would you go right on saying the things you always say?
Would life for you continue as it does from day to day?

Would your family conversation keep up its usual pace?
And would you find it hard each meal to say a table grace?
Would you sing the songs you always sing, and read the books you read
And let Him know the things on which your mind and spirit feed?
Would you take Jesus with you everywhere you'd planned to go?
Or would you, maybe, change your plans for just a day or so?

Would you be glad to have Him meet your very closest friends?
Or would you hope they'd stay away until His visit ends?
Would you be glad to have Him stay forever on and on?
Or would you sigh with great relief when He at last was gone?
It might be interesting to know the things that you would do,
If Jesus came in person to spend some time with you.

Author Unknown

THE FOUNTAIN OF LIFE

I have come to the Fountain of Life,
  A fountain that flows from above,
I have passed from the waters of strife,
  And come to the Elim of love.
I have drunk of Samaria's well,
  In the depths of my being it springs.
No mortal can measure or tell
  The gladness the Comforter brings.

I have come to the Fountain of Blood,
  That for guilt and uncleanness doth flow,
I have wash'd in its sin cleansing flood,
  And my garments are whiter than snow.
I count not my righteousness mine,
  'Tis Jesus that lives in my soul;
I partake of His nature divine,
  And in Him I am perfectly whole.

I have come to the Fountain of Love,
  He fills all the springs of my heart,
And enthroned there, all others above,
  Our friendship no power can part;
And so long as the fountain is full,
  The streams without measure must flow,
And the love that He pours in my soul
  To others in blessing must go.

Oh, come to the Fountain of Life,
  The fountain that never runs dry;
  Oh, drink of the boundless supply,
For God is the Fountain of Life.

--A. B. Simpson

(Permission Granted by Christian Publications, Inc.)

Love

ANTICIPATION

Perhaps this seems a foolish thing
Of long ago, young love and spring:
I saw my lover on the street,
And in my heart I felt a sweet
But wrenching pang, as suddenly
My heart went on ahead of me
To meet the heart of him halfway;
It seems it was but yesterday.

And now my life is nearly done.

I watch and wait and long for One
Who comes. O Lover of my soul,
It seems that I can scarce control
My eagerness. And suddenly
My heart goes on ahead of me,
I feel it leave my breast and soar
To meet Thee there at Heaven's door.

--Martha Snell Nicholson

NO EAST OR WEST

In Christ there is no East or West,
    In Him no South or North,
But one great Fellowship of Love
    Throughout the whole wide earth.

In Him shall true hearts everywhere
    Their high communion find.
His service is the golden cord
    Close-binding all mankind.

Join hands then, Brothers of the Faith,
    Whate'er your race may be!--
Who serves my Father as a son
    Is surely kin to me.

In Christ now meet both East and West,
    In Him meet South and North,
All Christly souls are one in Him,
    Throughout the whole wide earth.

--John Oxenham

I LOVE THEE, MY JESUS

What words can I find to tell Jesus I love Him
Because He first loved me?
Because of my ransom He paid with such suff'ring,
Upon the cursed tree.

O come, let us magnify Jesus together,
For praise becometh Thee;
And blessings about me I owe to my Saviour,
Who all things bought for me.

May never my praises be slow or be silent,
Nor e'er my love be dumb;
This sinner is saved and my sins all forgiven,
The Saviour's work is done!

O how can I love Thee enough, dear Redeemer,
How e'er repay my Friend?
I'll spread the glad sound of my praise and my heart love
On every joyful wind!

Chorus:
In the morning, at the noontime,
And when come ev'ning shadows,
I love Thee, my Jesus, I love Thee, my King.
In rejoicing and in sorrow,
In lightness and burden,
I love Thee, my Saviour and Lord.

--John R. Rice

A NUPTIAL WISH

"Dear friends, I scarce know what to say
On this important nuptial day.
I wish you joy; and while you live,
Such gifts as only God can give.
Whether life be short or long,
Dark with grief, or bright with song,
Whether sorrowful or glad,
Whether prosperous or sad,
Oh, that you, through Christ, may be
Heirs of immortality;--
Heirs of righteousness and peace,
Heirs of life that ne'er shall cease,
Heirs of glories yet to come,
Heirs of the Eternal Home!
In the valley, on the height,
In the darkness, in the light;
Still possessed of living grace,
Pressing on with eager pace;
Ever keeping Christ in view,
Meek and humble, just and true;
Helpers of each other's faith,
One in Him, in life and death;
By His Spirit taught and led,
By His grace and mercy fed,
Blessed and guarded by His love,
Till with Him you meet above."

--C. H. Spurgeon

47

HOW MUCH I OWE

When this passing world is done,
When has sunk yon glowing sun,
When we stand with Christ in glory,
Looking o'er life's finished story,
Then, Lord, shall I fully know--
Not till then--how much I owe.

When I stand before the throne,
Dressed in beauty not my own,
When I see Thee as Thou art,
Love Thee with unsinning heart,
Then, Lord, shall I fully know--
Not till then--how much I owe.

When the praise of Heaven I hear,
Loud as thunders to the ear,
Loud as many waters' noise,
Sweet as harp's melodious voice,
Then, Lord, shall I fully know--
Not till then--how much I owe.

Even on earth, as through a glass
Darkly, let Thy glory pass,
Make forgiveness feel so sweet,
Make Thy Spirit's help so meet.
Even on earth, Lord, make me know
Something of how much I owe.

--Robert Murray McCheyne
May, 1837

Love is the purification of the heart from self.
It strengthens and ennobles the character, gives
a higher motive and a nobler aim to every action
of life, and makes both man and woman coura-
geous. The power to love truly and devotedly is
the highest gift with which a human being can be
endowed; but is a sacred fire that must not be
burned to idols.   --Geraldine Endsor

THE SENTINEL

The morning is the gate of day,
  But ere you enter there
See that you set to guard it with
  The sentinel of prayer.
So shall God's grace your steps attend,
  But nothing else pass through
Save what can give the countersign;
  The Father's will for you.

When you have reached the end of day
  Where night and sleep await,
Set there the sentinel again
  To bar the evening's gate.
So shall no fear disturb your rest,
  No danger and no care.
For only peace and pardon pass
  The watchful guard of prayer.

--James G. Lawson
From the British Weekly

THE GOLDEN CORD

Through every minute of this day,
  Be with me, Lord!
Through every day of all this week,
  Be with me, Lord!
Through every week of all this year,
  Be with me, Lord!
Through all the years of all this life,
  Be with me, Lord!

So shall the days and weeks and years
Be threaded on a golden cord,
And all draw on with sweet accord
Unto Thy fulness, Lord,
That so, when time is past,
By grace, I may at last,
  Be with Thee, Lord.

-- John Oxenham

LORD, I HAVE SHUT THE DOOR

Lord, I have shut the door,
  Speak now the word
Which in the din and throng
  Could not be heard;
Hushed now my inner heart,
  Whisper Thy will,
While I have come apart,
  While all is still.

Lord, I have shut the door,
  Here do I bow;
Speak, for my soul attent
  Turns to Thee now.
Rebuke Thou what is vain,
  Counsel my soul,
Thy holy will reveal,
  My will control.

In this blest quietness
  Clamorings cease;
Here in Thy presence dwells
  Infinite peace;
Yonder the strife and cry,
  Yonder, the sin:
Lord, I have shut the door,
  Thou art within!

Lord, I have shut the door,
  Strengthen my heart;
Yonder awaits the task--
  I share a part.
Only through grace bestowed
  May I be true;
Here, while alone with Thee,
  My strength renew.

--William M. Runyan

A HAPPY DAY

Today will be a happy day
If, first, you find some time to pray;
If, first, alone you go apart
From worldly things, and in your heart
You make resolve to do your best
And then to God you leave the rest.
For God will take the hate and fear
Of yesterday and yesteryear
And in their place He'll make you feel
The light and love He would reveal;
Yes, this will be a happy day
If, friend, right now you'll stop and pray.

--Author unknown

JESUS, HEAR ME, TOO!

Thou didst hear the pleading leper,
Crying, "Jesus, if Thou wilt,
Thou canst make me clean,
Thou canst make me clean."
And Thou saidst, "I will," and "Be Thou clean."

In the upper room they waited,
Praying for the Holy Ghost,
And the pow'r came down,
And the pow'r came down;
And three thousand souls were saved that day.

In hard bondage down in Egypt,
Israel suffered and they prayed,
Thou didst hear their cry,
Didst not pass them by;
And to Canaan land they came at last.

In the jail were Paul and Silas,
Beaten, sore and fast in stocks,
But they sang and prayed,
Got the jailer saved;
God delivered them in mighty power.

Chorus:

Jesus, hear me; Saviour, hear me.
Let my sins be washed away,
And my heart made right, I pray.
Jesus, hear me; Saviour, hear me;
Let Thy Spirit and Thy blessing fall on me.

--John R. Rice

WAIT ON!

To talk with God,
No breath is lost --
Talk on!

To walk with God,
No strength is lost --
Walk on!

To wait on God,
No time is lost --
Wait on!

-- Author Unknown

SOME MINUTES IN THE MORNING

Some minutes in the morning,
  Ere the cares of life begin,
Ere the heart's wide door is open
  For the world to enter in.
Oh, then alone with Jesus,
  In the silence of the morn,
In heavenly, sweet communion
  Let your every day be born,
In the quietude that blesses,
  With a prelude of repose,
Let your soul be soothed and softened
  As the dew revives the rose.

Some minutes in the morning
  Take your Bible in your hand,
And catch a glimpse of glory
  From the peaceful promised land.
It will linger still before you
  When you seek the busy mart,
And like flowers of hope will blossom
  Into beauty in your heart.
The precious words like jewels
  Will glisten all the day
With a rare refulgent glory
  That will brighten all the way!

-- Selected

A QUIET PLACE

'Mid all the traffic of the ways,
  Turmoils without, within,
Make in my heart a quiet place,
  And come and dwell therein;

A little shrine of quietness,
  All sacred to Thyself,
Where Thou shalt all my soul possess,
  And I may find myself;

A little shelter from life's stress,
  Where I may lay me prone,
And bare my soul in loneliness,
  And know as I am known.

A little place of mystic grace,
  Of self and sin swept bare,
Where I may look upon Thy face,
  And talk with Thee in prayer.

--John Oxenham

AN HOUR WITH THEE

Lord, what a change within us one short hour
  Spent in Thy presence will avail to make!
  What heavy burdens from our bosoms take!
What parched grounds refresh as with a shower!
We kneel, and all around us seem to lower;
  We rise, and all the distant and the near,
  Stands forth in sunny outline, brave and clear;
We kneel, how weak; we rise, how full of power!
  Why, therefore, should we do ourselves this wrong,
  Or others -- that we are not always strong --
That we are sometimes overborne with care --
  That we should ever weak or heartless be,
Anxious or troubled -- when with us is prayer,
  And joy and strength and courage are with Thee?

-- Richard Chenevix Trench

THE MORNING WATCH

The early morn with Jesus;
  His happy, welcome guest!
The first glad thoughts for Jesus,
  The brightest and the best!

Alone, alone, with Jesus,
  No other may intrude,
The secrets of Jehovah,
  Are told in solitude.

This is the time to worship,
  This is the time for prayer;
The sweetest time for laying
  The heart's petitions bare.

The time for holy wrestling,
  The time to intercede;
The time to win from Jesus,
  The help and strength we need.

--Author Unknown

WHEN FATHER PRAYS

When father prays he doesn't use
  The words the preacher does;
There's different things for different days,
  But mostly it's for us.

When father prays the house is still,
  His voice is slow and deep.
We shut our eyes, the clock ticks loud,
  So quiet we must keep.

He prays that we may be good boys,
  And later on good men;
And then we squirm, and think we won't
  Have any quarrels again.

You'd never think, to look at Dad,
  He once had tempers, too.
I guess if father needs to pray,
  We youngsters surely do.

Sometimes the prayer gets very long
  And hard to understand,
And then I wiggle up quite close,
  And let him hold my hand.

I can't remember all of it,
  I'm little yet, you see;
But one thing I cannot forget,
  My father prays for me!

--Author Unknown

WORDS WITHOUT HEART?

I often say my prayers,
  But do I ever pray;
And do the wishes of my heart
  Go with the words I say?

I may as well kneel down
  And worship gods of stone
As offer to the living God
  A prayer of words alone.

For words without the heart
  The Lord will never hear;
Nor will He to those lips attend
  Whose prayers are not sincere.

--John Burton

ASK AND YE SHALL RECEIVE

O praying one, who long has prayed,
  And yet no answer heard,
Have ye been sometimes half afraid
  God might not keep His word?
Seems prayer to fall on deafened ears?
  Does Heaven seem blind and dumb?
Is hope deferred? Believe -- believe --
  The answer time will come!

"Ask what ye will" -- His Word is true,
  His power is all divine;
Ye cannot test His love too far;
  His utmost shall be thine.
God does not mock believing prayer;
  Ye shall not go unfed!
He gives no serpent for a fish,
  Nor gives He stones for bread.

Thy inmost longings may be told;
  The hopes that turned to shame,
The empty life, the thwarted plans;
  The good that never came.
Say not, "The promise is not mine,
  God did not hear me pray;
I prayed -- I trusted fully -- but
  The grave hath barred the way."

God heard thee -- He hath not forgot,
  Faith shall at length prevail;
Yea -- know it! Not one smallest jot
  Of all His word can fail.
For if ye truly have believed,
  Not vain hath been thy prayer!
As God is true, thy hope shall come --
  Sometime, someway, somewhere.

                --Mrs. Havens

LEAVE ME NOT!

Still let Thy wisdom be my guide,
  Nor take Thy flight from me away;
Still with me let Thy grace abide,
  That I from Thee may never stray.
Let Thy Word richly in me dwell,
  Thy peace and love my portion be;
My joy to endure and do Thy will,
  Till perfect I am found in Thee.

              --John Wesley

WHAT IS PRAYER?

Prayer is the soul's sincere desire,
  Utter'd or unexpress'd;
The motion of a hidden fire
  That trembles in the breast.

Prayer is the burthen of a sigh,
  The falling of a tear,
The upward glancing of the eye,
  When none but God is near.

Prayer is the simplest form of speech
  That infant lips can try;
Prayer the sublimest strains that reach
  The Majesty on high.

Prayer is the contrite sinner's voice
  Returning from his ways,
While angels in their songs rejoice,
  And cry,"Behold, he prays!"

Prayer is the Christian's vital breath,
  The Christian's native air;
His watchword at the gates of death;
  He enters Heaven with prayer.

The saints in prayer appear as one
  In word, and deed, and mind;
While with the Father and the Son
  Sweet fellowship they find.

No prayer is made by man alone:
  The Holy Spirit pleads;
And Jesus, on the eternal throne,
  For mourners intercedes.

O Thou, by whom we come to God!
  The Life, the Truth, the Way!
The path of prayer Thyself hast trod:
  Lord! teach us how to pray!

                                    --James Montgomery

BEGIN THE DAY WITH GOD

Every morning lean thine arms awhile
Upon the window-sill of Heaven
And gaze upon thy Lord,
Then, with the vision in thy heart,
Turn strong to meet thy day.

                    --Author Unknown

ERE YOU LEFT YOUR ROOM

Ere you left your room this morning,
  Did you think to pray?
In the name of Christ, our Saviour,
  Did you sue for loving favor,
As a shield today?

When your heart was filled with anger,
  Did you think to pray?
Did you plead for grace, my brother,
  That you might forgive another
Who had crossed your way?

When sore trials came upon you,
  Did you think to pray?
When your soul was full of sorrow,
  Balm of Gilead did you borrow
At the gates of day?

Chorus:

Oh, how praying rests the weary!
  Prayer will change the night to day;
So when life seems dark and dreary,
  Don't forget to pray.

                    --Mary A. Kidder

NO TIME TO PRAY

  No time to pray!
Oh, who so fraught with earthly care
As not to give to humble prayer
  Some part of day?

  No time to pray!
What heart so clean, so pure within,
That needeth not some check from sin,
  Needs not to pray?

  No time to pray!
'Mid each day's danger, what retreat
More needful than the mercy-seat?
  Who need not pray?

  No time to pray!
Then sure your record falleth short;
Excuse will fail you as resort,
  On that last day.

    What thought more drear,
Than that our God His face should hide,
And say through all life's swelling tide,
    No time to hear!

                    --Anonymous

Seasonal

THE INN THAT MISSED ITS CHANCE
(The Landlord Speaks -- 28 A.D.)

What could be done? The inn was full of folk:
His honor, Marcus Lucius, and his scribes
Who made the census; honorable men
From farthest Galilee, come hitherward
To be enrolled; high ladies and their lords;
The rich, the rabbis, such a noble throng
As Bethlehem has never seen before,
And may not see again. And there they were
Close herded with their servants, till the inn,
Was like a hive at swarming-time, and I
Was fairly crazed among them.

          Could I know
That they were so important? Just the two,
No servants, just a workman sort of man
Leading a donkey, and his wife thereon
Drooping and pale -- I saw them not myself,
My servants must have driven them away;
But had I seen them, how was I to know?
Were inns to welcome stragglers, up and down
In all our towns from Beersheba to Dan,
Till He should come? And how were men to know?
There was a sign, they say, a heavenly light
Resplendent, but I had no time for stars,
And there were songs of angels in the air

Out on the hills; but how was I to hear
Amid the thousand clamors of an inn?
Of course, if I had known them, who they were,
And who was He that should be born that night --
For now I learn that they will make Him King,
A second David, who will ransom us
From these Philistine Romans -- who but He
That feeds an army with a loaf of bread,
And if a soldier falls, He touches him
And up he leaps uninjured? Had I known,
I would have turned the whole inn upside down,
His honor, Marcus Lucius, and the rest,
And sent them all to the stables, had I known.

So you have seen Him, stranger, and perhaps
Again will see Him. Prithee say for me
I did' not know; and if He comes again,
As He will surely come, with retinue,
And banners, and an army, tell my Lord
That all my inn is His to make amends.

Alas, alas! to miss a chance like that!
This inn that might be chief among them all,
The birthplace of Messiah -- had I known!

          -- Amos R. Wells

CHRISTMAS EVERYWHERE

Everywhere, everywhere, Christmas tonight!
Christmas in lands of the fir-tree and pine,
Christmas in lands of the palm-tree and vine,
Christmas where snow peaks stand solemn and white,
Christmas where cornfields stand sunny and bright.
Christmas where children are hopeful and gay,
Christmas where old men are patient and gray,

Christmas where peace, like a dove in his flight,
Broods o'er brave men in the thick of the fight;
Everywhere, everywhere, Christmas tonight!

For the Christ-child who comes is the Master of all;
No palace too great, no cottage too small.

--Phillips Brooks

THAT NIGHT

That night when in the Judean skies
  The mystic star dispensed its light,
A blind man moved in his sleep --
  And dreamed that he had sight.

That night when shepherds heard the song
  Of hosts angelic choiring near,
A deaf man stirred in slumber's spell --
  And dreamed that he could hear!

That night when in the cattle stall
  Slept Child and mother cheek by jowl,
A cripple turned his twisted limbs --
  And dreamed that he was whole.

That night when o'er the newborn Babe
  The tender Mary rose to lean,
A loathsome leper smiled in sleep --
  And dreamed that he was clean.

That night when to the mother's breast
  The little King was held secure,
A harlot slept a happy sleep --
  And dreamed that she was pure!

That night when in the manger lay
  The Sanctified who came to save,
A man moved in the sleep of death --
  And dreamed there was no grave.

-- Author Unknown

MY NEW YEAR'S GIFT

Laid on Thine altar, O my Lord divine,
  Accept my gift this day, for Jesus' sake,
I have no jewels to adorn Thy shrine,
  Nor any world-famed sacrifice to make;
But here I bring within my trembling hands,
  This will of mine, a thing that seemeth small,
Yet Thou alone, O Lord, canst understand
  How when I yield Thee this, I yield my all.

Hidden therein Thy searching gaze can see
  Struggles of passion, visions of delight,
All that I have, or am, or fain would be,
  Deep loves, fond hopes, and longings infinite;
It hath been wet with tears, and dimmed with sighs,
  Clenched in my grasp, till beauty hath it none;
Now from Thy footstool, where it vanquished lies,
  The prayer ascendeth, "May Thy will be done."

Take it, O Father, ere my courage fail,
  And merge it so into Thine own will, that e'en
If in some desperate hour my cries prevail,
  And Thou give back my gift, it may have been
So changed, so purified, so fair have grown,
  So one with Thee, so filled with love divine,
I may not know or feel it as my own,
  But gaining back my will, may find it Thine.

-- Selected

MESSAGE OF THE NEW YEAR

I asked the New Year for some motto sweet,
Some rule of life with which to guide my feet;
I asked, and paused; he answered soft and low:
  "God's will to know."

"Will knowledge then suffice, New Year?" I cried;
And, ere the question into silence died,
The answer came: "Nay, but remember, too,
  God's will to do."

Once more I asked, "Is there no more to tell?"
And once again the answer sweetly fell:
"Yes! this one thing, all other things above,
  God's will to love."

--Anonymous

AUTUMN

The world puts on its robes of glory now;
  The very flowers are tinged with deeper dyes;
The waves are bluer, and the angels pitch
  Their shining tents along the sunset skies.

--Albert Leighton

THE HEAVENLY STRANGER

No warm, downy pillow His sweet head pressed;
No soft silken garments His fair form dressed;
 He lay in a manger,
 This Heavenly Stranger,
The precious Lord Jesus, the wonderful Child.

No jubilant clang of rejoicing bell
The glorious news to the world did tell;
 But angels from glory
 Sang sweetly the story
Of Bethlehem's Stranger, the Saviour of men.

Thou Heavenly Stranger, so gentle and mild,
Though born in a manger, the Father's own Child,
 We'll worship before Thee
 And praise and adore Thee,
And sing the glad story again and again.

--Ada Blenkhorn

NEW YEAR'S WISHES

What shall I wish thee! Treasures of earth?
Songs in the springtime, pleasures and mirth?
Flowers in thy pathway, skies ever clear?
Would this insure thee a happy new year?

What shall I wish thee? What can be found,
Bringing the sunshine all the year round?
Where is the treasure, lasting and dear,
That shall insure thee a happy new year?

Faith that increaseth, walking in light;
Hope that aboundeth, happy and bright;
Love that is perfect, casting out fear—
Those shall insure thee a happy new year.

Peace in the Saviour, rest at His feet,
Smile in His countenance, radiant and sweet;
Joy in His presence, Christ ever near—
This will insure thee a happy new year.

—Frances Ridley Havergal

Service and Soul Winning

REMEMBERING IN HEAVEN

Should I, up in Heaven,
  Remember the heartache,
All the pain and the cross,
  All the shame and the loss,
The reproach of the Saviour
  I'd borne in earth's conflict,
In Heaven I'd laugh at the cost!

Or if, on the gold streets,
  I think of earth "treasures,"
Of the things I had bought,
  Of the fame dearly sought;
I'd smile in my mansion,
  My gem-studded mansion --
In Heaven I'd smile, "They are naught!"

Should I, in the Glory,
  Remember a loved one,
One who walked by my side,
  But is lost and outside;
If I never had begged him
  To trust in the Saviour,
In Heaven I'd sit down and cry.

Oh, then, spread the message,
  The work He has given;
Never mind the world's praise,
  Nor possessions men crave.
But oh, for the Saviour
  Bring souls into Heaven,
And joy thru eternity's day!

Jesus' blood paid my ransom
  And I'm bound for Heaven,
But what will I think
  When rememb'ring in Heaven?

-- John R. Rice

A PLACE FOR EVERYONE

There is a niche provided
  For every man,
Each makes his contribution
  In God's great plan;
Let no one feel superfluous
  In that vast scheme,
However small and hidden
  His life may seem.

Some must go forth to battle,
  Some mind the camp;
Some cross the mighty billows,
  Some tend the lamp
And keep their lonely vigil
  Till break of day,
To guide some storm-tossed vessel
  Upon its way.

Some serve their generation,
  Some those unborn;
Some lose their lives in secret,
  Like buried corn;
Some sow their fields with weeping,
  Some reap the grain
And fill their barns with plenty
  From others' pain.

Dear Master, Thy appointments
  To me are sweet,
If I'm but for Thy service
  A vessel meet;
In labors more abundant,
  Or out of sight,
Thine openings and shuttings
  Are always right.

-- Max I. Reich

Richard Baxter gave his ideal of preaching:

" To preach as though he'd never preach again, and as a dying man to dying men!"   --W. B. K.

THE TIME IS SHORT

The time is short!
If thou wouldst work for God it must be now;
If thou wouldst win the garland for thy brow,
  Redeem the time.

With His reward
He comes; He tarries not; His day is near;
When men least look for Him will He be here;
  Prepare for Him!

—H. Bonar

MY CHUM

He stood at the crossroads all alone,
  With the sunrise in his face;
He had no fear for the path unknown;
  He was set for a manly race.
But the road stretched east, and the road stretched west;
There was no one to tell him which way was the best;
So my chum turned wrong and went down, down, down,
Till he lost the race and the victor's crown
And fell at last in an ugly snare,
Because no one stood at the crossroads there.

Another chum on another day
  At the selfsame crossroads stood;
He paused a moment to choose the way
  That would stretch to the greater good.
And the road stretched east, and the road streched west;
But I was there to show him the best;
So my chum turned right and went on and on,
Till he won the race and the victor's crown;
He came at last to the mansions fair,
Because I stood at the crossroads there.

Since then I have raised a daily prayer
That I be kept faithful standing there;
To warn the runners as they come,
And save my own or another's chum.

--Author Unknown

ONLY

Only a seed--but it chanced to fall
In a little cleft of a city wall,
And, taking root, grew bravely up,
Till a tiny blossom crowned its top.

Only a thought--but the work it wrought
Could never by tongue or pen be taught;
For it ran through a life, like a thread of gold,
And the life bore fruit, a hundredfold.

Only a word--but 'twas spoken in love
With a whispered prayer to the Lord above,
And the angels in Heaven rejoiced once more,
For a new-born soul "entered in by the door."

--Jessie Gordon

HOW LONG SHALL I GIVE?

"Go break to the needy sweet charity's bread;
For giving is living," the angel said.
"And must I be giving again and again?"
My peevish and pitiless answer ran.
"Oh, no," said the angel, piercing me through,
"Just give till the Master stops giving to you."

--Anonymous

HERE AM I

We should pray the Lord of Harvest,
"Reapers send into Thy field."
Few are reapers; white and wasting
Are the fields, how rich the yield.

Holy Father, send a seraph,
From the altar take a coal,
Cleanse my lips; I hear, "Whom shall I
Send to garner precious souls?"

Not four months away the harvest,
Fields are white: lift up your eyes.
Fruit for life eternal gather,
Rich the wages for such prize.

Pluck as embers from the burning
Souls for whom the Saviour died.
Oh, then send me, Christ of mercy,
To the doomed and lost outside.

Chorus:

Here am I! (O Lord, send me)
Here am I! (I wait on Thee)
Send me forth, O Lord of Harvest,
Breathe on me Thy Holy Spirit.
Here am I! (O Lord, send me)
Here am I! (I wait on Thee)
Send me forth to win some precious soul today.

-- John R. Rice

THE MOTHER'S PRAYER

Lord, give me this soul!
I have waked for it when I should have slept,
I have yearned over it, and I have wept,
Till in my own the thought of it held sway
All through the night and day.

Lord, give me this soul!
If I might only lift its broken strands,
To lay them gently in Thy loving hands--
If I might know it had found peace in Thee,
What rest, what peace to me!

Thou wilt give me this soul!
Else why the joy, the grief, the doubt, the pain,
The thought perpetual, the one refrain,
The ceaseless longing that upon Thy breast
The tempest-tossed may rest?
Dear Lord, give me this soul!

--Author Unknown

A preacher who was popular with his congregation explained his successes as the result of a silent prayer he offered each time he entered the pulpit. It went like this:

"Lord, fill my mouth with worthwhile stuff, and nudge me when I've said enough!"

--School Activities

THE PRICE OF REVIVAL

The price of revival, the cost of soul winning,
The long hours of praying, the burden, the tears;
The pleading with sinners, though lonely, a stranger,
Is repaid at the reaping up there.

The Saviour will see the travail of His soul
And be satisfied fully o'er souls He's redeemed;
Compared to that reaping, He scorned all His suff'ring,
To be paid at the reaping up there.

The treasures of earth, oh, how vain and how fleeting!
They vanish like mist and they wither like leaves;
But souls who are won by our tears and our pleading
Will remain for our reaping up there.

To come to that reaping with wood, hay, and stubble!
How sad to appear at the Lord's judgment seat,
With no one we've won to trust Jesus our Saviour
To present at the reaping up there.

The wise, they shall shine like the firmament glory,
When payday shall come for the winner of souls!
Then they who've saved many by salvation's story
Like the stars, blest forever, shall shine.

Reaping--heavenly reaping!
For souls won down here.

--John R. Rice

A PASSION FOR SOULS

Oh, for a passionate passion for souls!
  Oh, for a pity that yearns!
Oh, for the love that loves unto death!
  Oh, for the fire that burns!
Oh, for the pure prayer power that prevails,
  That pours itself out for the lost;
Victorious prayer in the Conqueror's name;
  Oh, for a Pentecost!

--Amy Carmichael

Paul said he was glad to have the Gospel preached, whatever might be the motive of the preacher. I thank God for the Gospel, whether it is preached on the street corner, under a brush arbor, in a tent, in the pulpit, or over the radio. It is not where the Gospel is preached that is the power of God unto salvation. I believe in credentials and in decency and in order. But God didn't say if somebody who has credentials preaches the Gospel it will save people. He said that it is the Gospel which does the business. The preacher is human, but the Gospel is divine. Men may resist a preacher, but they cannot resist the Gospel without doing it at the peril of their souls.

--Bob Jones, Sr.

THE GAMBLER'S WIFE

Dark is the night! How dark! No light! No fire!
Cold on the hearth, the last faint sparks expire!
Shivering, she watches, by the cradle side,
For him who pledged her love--last year a bride!

"Hark! 'tis his footstep! No!--'tis past!--'tis gone!"
Tick!--Tick!--"How wearily the time crawls on!
Why should he leave me thus?--He once was kind!
And I believed 'twould last!--How mad!--How blind!

"Rest thee, my babe!--Rest on!--'tis hunger's cry!
Sleep!--For there is no food!--The fount is dry!
Famine and cold, their wearying work have done;
My heart must break! And thou!" The clock strikes one.

"Hush! 'tis the dice-box! Yes! he's there! he's there!
For this!--for this he leaves me to despair!
Leaves love! leaves truth! his wife! his child! for what?
The wanton's smile--the villain--and the sot!

"Yet I'll not curse him. No! 'tis all in vain!
'Tis long to wait, but sure he'll come again!
And I could starve, and bless him but for you,
My child!--his child! Oh, fiend!" The clock strikes two.

"Hark! How the signboard creaks! The blast howls by.
Moan! moan! A dirge swells through the cloudy sky!
Ha! 'tis his knock! he comes!--he comes once more!"
'Tis but the lattice flaps! Thy hope is o'er!

"Can he desert us thus? He knows I stay
Night after night, in loneliness, to pray
For his return--and yet he sees no tear!
No! no! It can not be! He will be here!

"Nestle more closely, dear one, to my heart!
Thou'rt cold! Thou'rt freezing! But we will not part!
Husband!--I die!--Father!--It is not he!
O God! protect my child!" The clock strikes three.

They're gone, they're gone, the glimmering spark hath fled!
The wife and child are numbered with the dead.
On the cold earth, outstretched in solemn rest,
The babe lay, frozen on its mother's breast;
The gambler came at last--but all was o'er,
Dread silence reigned around. The clock struck four.

--T. DeWitt Talmage

WANDERED

The wind blows shrill along the hill,
--Black is the night and cold--
The sky hangs low with its weight of snow,
And the drifts are deep on the wold.
But what care I for wind or snow?
And what care I for the cold?
   Oh . . . where is my lamb--
   My one ewe lamb--
   That strayed from the fold?

The beasts are safely gathered in,
--Black is the night and cold--
They are snug and warm, and safe from harm,
In stall and byre and fold.
And the dogs and I, by the blazing fire,
Care nought for the snow and the cold.
   Oh . . . where is my lamb--
   My one ewe lamb--
   That strayed from the fold?

The barns are bursting with their store
Of grain like yellow gold;
A full, fat year has brought good cheer,
--Black is the night and cold--
But . . . what care I for teeming barns?
And what care I for gold?
   Oh . . . where is my lamb--
   My one ewe lamb--
   That strayed from the fold?

In the great kitchen, maids and men,
--Black is the night and cold--
Laugh loud and long, with jest and song,
And merry revel hold.
Let them laugh and sing, let them have their fling,
But for me--I am growing old.
   Oh . . . where is my lamb--
   My one ewe lamb--
   That strayed from the fold?

The old house moans, and sighs and groans,
--Black is the night and cold--
We have seen brave times, you and I, old friend,
But now--we are growing old.
We have stood foursquare to many a storm,
But now--we are growing old.
   Oh . . . where is my lamb--
   My one ewe lamb--
   That strayed from the fold?

Her mother sleeps on the hill out there,
--Black is the night and cold--
She is free from care, she is happier there,
Beneath the warm brown mould.
And I've sometimes hoped they may have met,
And the end of the tale be told.
   Ah . . . where is our lamb--
   Our one ewe lamb--
   That strayed from the fold?

Was that a branch that shed its load?
--Black is the night and cold--
Or--was it a footstep in the snow--
A timid footstep--halting, slow?
Ah me! I am getting old!
Is that a tapping--soft and low?
Can it be . . . I thought I heard . . . but no,
'Twas only a branch that shed its snow--
God's truth! I am getting old!
   For I thought . . . maybe
   It was my lamb
   Come home again to the fold.

Dear Lord! a hand at the frozen pane!
--White on the night's black cold--
O my lamb! my lamb! Are you come again?
My dear lost lamb, are you come again?
Are you come again to the fold?
It is! . . . It is! . . . Now I thank Thee, Lord,
For Thy mercies manifold!
   She is come again!
   She is home again!
   My lamb that strayed from the fold!

                --John Oxenham

A woman told Billy Sunday that she had a bad temper, but it was over in a minute. "So is a shotgun, but it blows everything to pieces," was his reply.   --Selected

"THE LIFTER OF MINE HEAD"

I have failed again! My courage gone,
  It seems no use to try.
I hear my old accuser say,
  "The soul that sins must die.
Is this the first time you have slipped
  Since Christ as Lord you named?
No! You have sinned time and again
  And you should be ashamed."

My head bent low, I bow in grief
  And know, too well, the truth
A faltering, stumbling sinner, I,
  And have been since my youth--
How can I face my Lord again,
  Or ask forgiveness sweet?
Do I presume that He would hear
  About the mercy seat?

Oh Thou, the Lifter of mine head,
  Sustain me once again,
Sufficiency is all from Thee,
  And self esteem is vain.
I am a willful child of Thine,
  The flesh indeed is weak.
Lift up mine head, O Lord, my God,
  Restore me while I speak!

                --Anonymous

CHRIST AT THE DOOR

In the silent midnight watches,
　List! thy bosom door!
How it knocketh - knocketh - knocketh—
　Knocketh evermore!
Say not 'tis thy pulse is beating:
　'Tis thy heart of sin;
'Tis thy Saviour knocks and crieth,
　"Rise and let me in."

Death comes on with reckless footsteps,
　To the hall and hut,
Think you, Death will tarry knocking
　Where the door is shut?
Jesus waiteth - waiteth - waiteth,
　But the door is fast;
Grieved, away thy Saviour goeth:
　Death breaks in at last.

Then 'tis time to stand entreating
　Christ to let thee in;
At the gate of Heaven beating,
　Waiting for thy sin.
Nay, alas! thou guilty creature:
　Hast thou then forgot?
Jesus waited long to know thee,
　Now He knows thee not.

Author Unknown

MERCY FOR ME?

Depth of mercy! can there be
Mercy still reserved for me?
Can my God His wrath forbear--
Me, the chief of sinners, spare?

I have long withstood His grace,
Long provoked Him to His face,
Would not hearken to His calls,
Grieved Him by a thousand falls.

Now incline me to repent;
Let me now my sins lament;
Now my foul revolt deplore;
Weep, believe, and sin no more.

There for me the Saviour stands,
Holding forth His wounded hands;
God is love! I know, I feel,
Jesus weeps and loves me still.

--Charles Wesley

COUNTED WORTHY

"Rejoicing that they were counted worthy to suffer"--Acts 5:41.
"If so be that we suffer with him, that we may be also glorified together"--Romans 8:17.

This weighty burden thou dost bear,
  This heavy cross,
It is a gift the Lord bestows,
  And not a loss;
It is a trust that He commits
  Unto thy care,
A precious lesson He has deigned
  With thee to share.
Rejoice that He so honors thee
  And so esteems,

That He should give into thy hands
  The things He deems
Of highest worth; the crown of thorns
  With Him to wear,
And all the suffering of that crown
  With Him to bear,
That by and by His glory, too,
  With Him thou'lt share.

--Annie Johnson Flint

IN NARROW WAYS

Some lives are set in narrow ways,
By Love's wise tenderness.
They seem to suffer all their days
Life's direst storm and stress.
But God shall raise them up at length,
His purposes are sure,
He for their weakness shall give strength,
For every ill a cure.

-- John Oxenham

THE VALUE OF A THORN

"Lest I should be exalted above measure
through the abundance of the revelations, there
was given to me a thorn in the flesh, the mes-
senger of Satan to buffet me, lest I should be
exalted above measure." --II Cor. 12:7

STRANGE GIFT INDEED! A thorn to prick,
To pierce into the very quick,
To cause perpetual sense of pain;
Strange gift--and yet, 'twas given for gain.
Unwelcome, yet it came to stay,
Nor could it e'en be prayed away.
It came to fill its God-planned place.
A life-enriching means of grace.

God's grace-thorns--oh, what forms they take;
What piercing, smarting pain they make!
And yet, each one in love is sent,
And always just for blessing meant.
And so, whate'er thy thorn may be
From God, accept it willingly;
But reckon Christ, His life, His power
To keep in thy most trying hour.

And sure, thy life will richer grow;
He grace sufficient will bestow.
And, in Heav'ns' morn, thy joy 'twill be
That, by His thorn, He strengthened thee.

--J. Danson Smith

THY HANDS, THY FEET

Lord, when I am weary with toiling,
And burdensome seem Thy commands,
If my load should lead to complaining,
Lord, show me Thy Hands--
Thy nail-pierced Hands, Thy cross-torn Hands,
My Saviour, show me Thy Hands.

Christ, if ever my footsteps should falter,
And I be prepared for retreat,
If desert or thorn cause lamenting,
Lord, show me Thy Feet--
Thy bleeding Feet, Thy nail-scarred Feet,
My Jesus, show me Thy Feet.

O God, dare I show Thee
My hands and my feet.

--Brenton Thoburn Bradley

God pity those who cannot say
"Not mine, but Thine"; who only pray,
"Let this cup PASS," and cannot see
The purpose in Gethsemane.

--Ella W. Wilcox

GOD IS IN EVERY TOMORROW

God is in every tomorrow,
  Therefore I live for today;
Certain of finding at sunrise
  Guidance and strength for the day,
Power for each moment of weakness,
  Hope for each moment of pain,
Comfort for every sorrow,
  Sunshine and joy after rain.

God is in every tomorrow,
  Planning for you and for me,
E'en in the dark I will follow,
  Trust where my eyes cannot see,
Stilled by His promise of blessing,
  Soothed by the touch of His hand,
Confident in His protection,
  Knowing my life-path is planned.

God is in every tomorrow,
  Life with its changes may come,
He is behind and before me,
  While in the distance shines Home.
Home--where no thoughts of tomorrow
  Ever can shadow my brow,
Home in the presence of Jesus,
  Through all Eternity now!

--Author Unknown

"Man," said one Christian Scotsman to another, "I got a wonderful text in my reading lesson today." "Oh," said his friend, "let me hear it." "Well," responded the other enthusiastically, " the text is Psalm 56:3, and it says, 'What time I am afraid, I will trust in Thee.' " "Very good," agreed his friend, smiling, "but I got a better text in my reading lesson, for in Isaiah 12:2, I read, 'I will trust, and not be afraid.' "

--Moody Monthly

AMEN!

I cannot say,
Beneath the pressure of life's care today
   I joy in these;
   But I can say
That I had rather walk this rugged way,
   If "Him" I please.

I cannot feel
That all is well, when darkening clouds conceal
   The shining sun;
   But then I know
God lives and loves; and say since it is so,
   " Thy will be done."

I cannot speak
In happy tones; the teardrops on my cheek
   Show I am sad;
   But I can speak
Of grace to suffer with submission meek,
   Until made glad.

I do not see
Why God should e'en permit some things to be
   When He is love;
   But I can see,
Though often dimly, through the mystery,
   His hand above.

I do not know
Where falls the seed that I have tried to sow
   With greatest care;
   But I shall know,
The meaning of each waiting hour below,
   Sometime, somewhere!

I do not look
Upon the present, nor in nature's book
   To read my fate;
   But I do look
For promised blessings in "God's holy Book,"
   And I can wait.

I may not try
To keep the hot tears back, but hush that sigh,
   "It might have been!"
   And try to still
Each rising murmur, and to God's sweet will
   Respond --- AMEN.

    --Ophelia G. Browning

WILT LOVE ME? TRUST ME? PRAISE ME?

O thou beloved child of My desire,
Whether I lead thee through green valleys,
   By still waters,
   Or through fire,
Or lay thee down in silence under snow,
Through any weather, and whatever
   Cloud may gather,
   Or wind may blow--
Wilt love Me? trust Me? praise Me?

No gallant bird, O dearest Lord, am I,
That anywhere, in any weather,
   Rising singeth;
   Low I lie.
And yet I cannot fear, for I shall soar;
Thy love shall wing me, blessed Saviour;
   So I answer,
   I adore, .
I love Thee, trust Thee, praise Thee.

--Amy Carmichael
in *Toward Jerusalem*

FRET NOT THYSELF

Far in the future
Lieth a fear,
Like a long, low mist of grey,
Gathering to fall in dreary rain;
Thus doth thy heart within thee complain;
And even now thou art afraid, for round thy dwelling
The flying winds are ever telling
Of the fear that lieth grey,
Like a gloom of brooding mist upon the way.

   But the Lord is always kind;
   Be not blind,
   Be not blind,
   To the shining of His face,
   To the comforts of His grace.
   Hath He ever failed thee yet?
   Never, never. Wherefore fret?
   Oh, fret not thyself, nor let
   Thy heart be troubled,
   Neither let it be afraid.

--Amy Carmichael
in *Toward Jerusalem*

The promises of the Bible are very large; you can lie down and stretch out on them and you can't kick the footboard, scratch the headboard, or touch the railing on either side.
      --Bud Robinson

ALL YOUR ANXIETY

Is there a heart o'erbound by sorrow?
  Is there a life weighed down by care?
Come to the cross, each burden bearing,
  All your anxiety--leave it there.

No other Friend so keen to help you;
  No other Friend so quick to hear;
No other place to leave your burden;
  No other One to hear your prayer.

Come then, at once, delay no longer;
  Heed His entreaty, kind and sweet;
You need not fear a disappointment,
  You shall find peace at the mercy-seat.

All your anxiety, all your care,
Bring to the mercy-seat, leave it there;
Never a burden He cannot bear,
  Never a Friend like Jesus.

--Lieut. Col. E. H. Joy

STEP BY STEP

He does not lead me year by year
Nor even day by day.
But step by step my path unfolds;
My Lord directs my way.

Tomorrow's plans I do not know,
I only know this minute;
But He will say, "This is the way,
By faith now walk ye in it."

And I am glad it is so.
Today's enough to bear;
And when tomorrow comes, His grace
Shall far exceed its care.

What need to worry then, or fret?
The God who gave His Son
Holds all my moments in His hand
And gives them, one by one.

--Barbara C. Ryberg

I'M LEANING ON JESUS

Cast all your care on Him, He careth for you;
His promise is given, His Word it is true;
He clotheth the lilies, the sparrows He feeds,
So tell Him your burdens and needs.

God spared not His Son, but delivered Him up;
To pay our transgressions, no price was too much;
How shall He not with Him give all things indeed?
So boldly His mercy we plead.

How large is your burden? Then make loud your call!
Resources are boundless, His power, His all
Are pledged, He exceeding abundant will prove;
Your mountains He's able to move.

Lean on Him in sorrow, in poverty's woes;
He feels our temptations, in pity He knows;
The Father His children in mercy doth hear,
And lifts up the fallen ones dear.

Chorus:

I'm leaning on Jesus,
He walks with me over life's road;
I'm leaning on Jesus,
He carries, He carries my load.

--John R. Rice

THIS I KNOW

I do not know what next may come
  Across my pilgrim way;
I do not know tomorrow's road,
  Nor see beyond today.
But this I know--my Saviour knows
  The path I cannot see;
And I can trust His wounded hand
  To guide and care for me.

I do not know what may befall,
  Of sunshine or of rain;
I do not know what may be mine,
  Of pleasure and of pain;
But this I know--my Saviour knows,
  And whatsoe'er it be,
Still I can trust His love to give
  What will be best for me.

I do not know what may await,
  Or what the morrow brings;
But with the glad salute of faith,
  I hail its opening wings:
For this I know--that in my Lord
  Shall all my needs be met;
And I can trust the heart of Him
  Who has not failed me yet.

--E. Margaret Clarkson

IF I COULD CHOOSE MY WAY

IF I could choose my way,
And chart my course down life's uncertain sea,
Perhaps, O loving Lord, it would not be
The course which Thou in love had planned for me.
I'd shun, perhaps, the dark and dangerous deep,
And strive along the shallow shore to keep,
To drift, by gentle breezes lulled to sleep--
If I could have my way.

And having my own way,
I'd never know Thy wonder-working pow'r,
Thy strength, Thy grace in life's most trying hour,
When death stood waiting, ready to devour.
I'd never know the thrill of Thy sweet voice
That bid me in the darkness to rejoice.
How much, O Lord, I'd lose, were mine the choice--
If I could have my way.

If I could have my way--
O Jesus, were that pow'r giv'n to me,
I'd dare not choose a path apart from Thee.
Be Thou my guide, where'er Thy way may be.
Safe in Thy love, I fear no rocks ahead;
The wild and boisterous billows bear no dread.
No way but Thine, dear Lord, would I be led.
Choose Thou my way.

--Avis B. Christiansen

HE MAKETH NO MISTAKE

My Father's way may twist and turn,
My heart may throb and ache,
But in my soul I'm glad I know
He maketh no mistake.
My cherished plans may go astray,
My hopes may fade away,
But still I'll trust my Lord to lead
For He doth know the way.
Tho' night be dark and it may seem
That day will never break;
I'll pin my faith, my all in Him,
He maketh no mistake.
There's so much now I cannot see,
My eyesight's far too dim;
But come what may, I'll simply trust
And leave it all to Him.
For by and by the mist will lift
And plain it all He'll make,
Through all the way, tho' dark to me,
He made not one mistake.

--A. M. Overton

THE DAY--THE WAY

Not for one single day
Can I discern my way,
But this I surely know,--
Who gives the day,
Will show the way,
So I securely go.

--John Oxenham

A PRAYER FOR PATIENCE

Grant us, O Lord, the grace to bear
  The littly prickly thorns;
The hasty words that seem unfair;
  The jest that makes our weakness plain;
The cherished plan o'erturned;
  The careless touch upon our pain;
The slight we have not earned;
  The rasp of care, dear Lord, today,
Lest all these fretful things
  Make needless grief; O give, we pray
The heart that trusts and sings.

                --Julia W. Wolfe

"In the world ye shall have tribulation; but
be of good cheer; I have overcome the world."

"There are deep things of God. Push out from shore.
Hast thou found much? Give thanks and look for more.
Dost fear the generous Giver to offend?
Then know His store of bounty hath no end.
He doth not need to be implored or teased;
The more we take, the better He is pleased."

Beside the common inheritance of the land, there are
some special possessions.

                --A. B. Simpson

THE FAULT IS MINE

Sometimes God seems so far away,
  The mists between so dense,
My heart is filled with sudden dread,
  Foreboding, and suspense.

The very prayers I utter
  Come straightway back through space--
Too weak to make their faltering way
  Up to the throne of grace.

And then again, God seems so near,
  I cannot but believe;
His faintest whisper rings as clear
  As vesper chimes at eve.

"I never leave thee nor forsake,"
  His gentle whisper saith;
And what had caused my sudden dread
  Was just my lack of faith!

              --Edith M. Lee

I do not ask my cross to understand,
  My way to see;
Better in the darkness just to feel Thy hand
  And follow Thee.

              --Adelaide Proctor.

LIKE A RIVER GLORIOUS

Like a river glorious is God's perfect peace,
Over all victorious in its bright increase;
Perfect, yet it floweth fuller every day;
Perfect, yet it groweth deeper all the way.

Hidden in the hollow of His blessed hand,
Never foe can follow, never traitor stand;

Not a surge of worry, not a shade of care,
Not a blast of hurry touch the spirit there.

Every joy or trial falleth from above
Traced upon our dial by the Sun of Love.
We may trust Him fully, all for us to do;
They who trust Him wholly find Him wholly true.

--Frances R. Havergal

GOD'S PLAN

God moves in a mysterious way,
    His wonders to perform;
He plants His footsteps in the sea,
    And rides upon the storm.

Deep in unfathomable mines
    Of never-failing skill,
He treasures up His bright designs
    And works His sov'reign will.

Ye fearful saints, fresh courage take,
    The clouds ye so much dread
Are hid with mercy, and shall break
    In blessing on your head.

Judge not the Lord by feeble sense,
    But trust Him for His grace;
Behind a frowning providence
    He hides a smiling face.

His purposes will ripen fast,
    Unfolding every hour;
The bud may have a bitter taste,
    But sweet will be the flower.

Blind unbelief is sure to err,
    And scan His work in vain;
God is His own interpreter,
    And He will make it plain.

--William Cowper, 1731-1800

80

THROUGH FAITH

Through faith we understand
  The things we cannot know--
The hidden pattern God has planned,
  And why each thread is so;
We trace life's vast design
  And lose His golden strand,
But when our wills with His entwine
  Through faith we understand.

Through faith we understand
  What to our sight is dim,
And still Love's sweet, all-knowing hand
  Leads those who trust in Him.
Ours not to know the way,
  But bow to His command;
And when our child-like hearts obey,
  Through faith we understand.

                    -- E. Margaret Clarkson

The saints should never be dismay'd,
  Nor sink in hopeless fear!
For when they least expect His aid,
  The Saviour will appear.

Wait for His seasonable aid,
  And though it tarry, wait:
The promise may be long delay'd
  But cannot come too late.

                    --Cowper.

BY FAITH AND NOT BY SIGHT

I walk by faith and not by sight,
Why seek along the way for light
  Beyond today?
The Saviour holds my feeble hand,
And so I follow His command;
  He is my stay.

I need not look beyond to see,
I need not know His way for me
  Beyond this hour
For by His grace His will I'll do,
His gracious Spirit leads me through,
  And gives me power.

                    --Eva Gray

SHUT WINDOWS

When the outer eye grows dim,
Turns the inner eye to Him,
  Who makes darkness light.
Fairer visions you may see,
Live in nobler company,
And in larger liberty,
  Than the men of sight.

He sometimes shuts the windows but to open hidden doors,
Where all who will may wander bold and free,
For His house has many mansions, and the mansions many floors,
And every room is free to you and me.

                    --John Oxenham

DRIFTING AWAY FROM GOD

Drifting away from Christ in thy youth,
Drifting away from mercy and truth,
Drifting to sin in tenderest youth,
    Drifting away from God!

Drifting away from mother and home,
Drifting away in sorrow to roam,
Drifting where peace and rest cannot come,
    Drifting away from God!

Drifting away on sin's treach'rous tide,
Drifting where death and darkness abide,
Drifting from Heav'n away in your pride,
    Drifting away from God!

Drifting away from hope's blessed shore,
Drifting away where wild breakers roar;
Drifted and stranded, wrecked, evermore,
    Far from the light of God!

Why will you drift on billows of shame,
Spurning His grace again and again?
Soon you'll be lost! In sin to remain,
    Ever away from God!

Brother, the Saviour has called you before;
See! you are nearing eternity's shore!
Soon you may perish, be lost evermore,
    Jesus now calls for you!

--Mrs. J. A. Griffith

EVEN SO, COME QUICKLY!

The Prince of Peace came down to earth
  With God's goodwill to men,
And all the hosts of Heaven sang,
And high their hallelujahs rang
  O'er sleeping Bethlehem;
But men heard not the songs of love
  For tumult of earth's strife:
High on a hill they hewed a tree,
Carried their King to Calvary,
  And slew the Lord of Life.

The Prince of Peace looks down on earth,
  Sick with the strife of sin,
And watches men wage warfare blind
The while He yearns to help them find
  The Peace He died to win.
War rages on in savage hate
  With spectred horrors grim:
Distracted earth is sore distressed,
And prays for peace and cries for rest,
  But will have none of Him.

The Prince of Peace shall come to earth
  And earth shall own His sway;
Not thorn, but glory on His brow,
Earth's every knee to Him shall bow
  In that triumphal day.

His righteous rule shall know no end;
  Wars shall forever cease;
But not till comes her Saviour King,
Love's banner o'er His world to fling,
  Shall rebel earth have Peace!

--E. Margaret Clarkson

THE ALTAR

A broken ALTAR, Lord, Thy servant rears,
Made of a heart, and cemented with tears:
Whose parts are as Thy hand did frame;
No workman's tool hath touch'd the same.
          A HEART alone
          Is such a stone,
          As   nothing but
          Thy power doth cut.
          Wherefore each part
          Of my hard heart
          Meets in this frame,
          To praise Thy name.
That if I chance   to hold my peace,
These stones to praise Thee may not cease.
O let Thy blessed SACRIFICE be mine,
And sanctify this ALTAR to be Thine.

-- George Herbert

THE WORLD IS MINE

Today upon a bus, I saw a lovely girl with golden hair.
I envied her—she seemed so gay—and wished I were as fair.
When suddenly she rose to leave, I saw her hobble down the aisle;
She had one leg, and wore a crutch: But as she passed—a smile!
    Oh, God forgive me when I whine.
    I have two legs. The world is mine!

And then I stopped to buy some sweets. The lad who sold them had such charm.
I talked with him. He seemed so glad. If I were late 'twould do no harm.
And as I left he said to me: "I thank you. You have been so kind.
It's nice to talk with folks like you. You see," he said, "I'm blind.
    Oh, God forgive me when I whine.
    I have two eyes. The world is mine!

Later, while walking down the street, I saw a child with eyes of blue.
He stood and watched the others play. It seemed he knew not what to do.
I stopped a moment, then I said: "Why don't you join the others, dear?"
He looked ahead without a word, and then I knew he could not hear.
    Oh, God forgive me when I whine.
    I have two ears. The world is mine!

With feet to take me where I'd go,
With eyes to see the sunset's glow,
With ears to hear what I would know—
    Oh, God forgive me when I whine.
    I'm blessed indeed. The world is mine.

--Author Unknown

TOMORROW

He was going to be all that a mortal could be--
      Tomorrow;
No one would be kinder nor braver than he--
      Tomorrow;
  A friend who was troubled and weary he knew
  Who'd be glad of a lift and who needed it, too;
  On him he would call and see what he could do--
      Tomorrow.

Each morning he stacked up the letters he'd write--
      Tomorrow;
And he thought of the folks he would fill with delight--
      Tomorrow;
  It was too bad, indeed, he was busy today,
  And hadn't a minute to stop on his way;
  "More time I would have to give others," he'd say--
      "Tomorrow."

The greatest of workers this man would have been--
      Tomorrow;
The world would have known him had he ever seen--
      Tomorrow;
  But the fact is he died, and he faded from view,
  And all that he left here when living was through
  Was a mountain of things he intended to do--
      Tomorrow.

           --Anonymous.

WHICH ONE?

One of us, dear--
  But one--
Will sit by the bed with marvelous fear,
  And clasp the hand
Growing cold as it feels for the spirit land--
  Darling, which one?

One of us, dear--
  But one--
Will stand by the other's coffin bier,
  And look and weep,
While those marble lips strange silence keep--
  Darling, which one?

One of us, dear--
  But one--
By an open grave will drop a tear,
  And homeward go,
The anguish of an unshared grief to know--
  Darling, which one?

One of us, darling, it must be.
  It may be you will slip from me:
Or perhaps my life may first be done:
  I'm glad we do not know
  Which one.

           --Selected

THEY SAID, "The Master is coming
    To honor the town today,
And no one can tell at whose house or home
    The Master will choose to stay."
And I thought, while my heart beat wildly,
    "What if He should come to mine.
How I would strive to entertain
    And honor the Guest Divine!"

And straight I turned to toiling
    To make my home more neat;
I swept and polished and garnished,
    And decked it with blossoms sweet.
I was troubled for fear the Master
    Might come e'er my task was done,
So I hastened and worked the faster,
    And watched the hurrying sun.

But right in the midst of my duties
    A woman came to my door.
She had come to tell me her sorrows,
    And my comfort and aid to implore.
And I said, "I cannot listen
    Nor help you any today;
I have greater things to tend to,"
    And the pleader turned away.

But soon there came another,--
    A cripple, thin, pale and grey,--
And said, "Let me stop and rest
    Awhile in your house, I pray.
I have travelled far since morning.
    I am hungry, faint and weak;
My heart is full of misery,
    And comfort and help I seek."

And I cried, "I am grieved and sorry,
    But I cannot help you today.
I look for a Great and Noble Guest,"
    And the cripple went away;
And the day wore swiftly onward,--
    My tasks were almost done,
And a prayer was ever in my heart
    That to me the Master might come.

And I thought I would spring to meet Him,
    And serve Him with utmost care,
When a little child stood by me,
    With a face so sweet and fair--
Sweet but with the marks of teardrops--
    And his clothes were tattered and old;
A finger was bruised and bleeding,
    And his little bare feet were cold.

IS COMING

And I said, "I am sorry for you,
  You are sorely in need of care;
But I cannot stop to give it,
  You must hasten on elsewhere."
And at the words a shadow
  Swept over his blue-veined brow,--
"Someone will feed and clothe you, dear,
  But I am too busy now."

At last the day was ended,
  And my toil was over and done;
My house was swept and garnished,
  And I watched in the dusk --alone--
Watched, but no footfall sounded,
  No one paused at my gate;
No one entered my cottage door,
  I could only pray, and wait.

I waited till night had deepened,--
  And the Master had not come.
"He has entered some other door," I cried,
  "And gladdened some other home!
My labor has been for nothing,"
  And I bowed my head and wept.
My heart was sore with longing--
  Yet in spite of it all I slept.

Then the Master stood before me;
  And His face was grave and fair;
"Three times today I stopped at your house
  And craved your pity and care;
Three times you sent me onward,
  Unhelped and uncomforted;
And the blessing you might have had was lost,
  And your chance to serve has fled."

"O Lord, dear Lord, forgive me!
  How could I know it was Thee?"
My soul was shamed and bowed
  In the depths of humility.
And He said, "Thy sin is pardoned,
  But the blessing is lost to thee;
For in comforting not the least of Mine,
  Ye have failed to comfort me."

                    --Emma A. Lent

I remember hearing a young convert who got up to say something for Christ in the open air. Not being accustomed to speaking, he stammered a good deal at first, when an infidel came right along and shouted out, "Young man, you ought to be ashamed of yourself, standing and talking like that." "Well," the young man replied, "I'm ashamed of myself, but I'M NOT ASHAMED OF CHRIST." That was a good answer.   --Moody

87

ON THE SUMMIT

The path was steep and snowy--the way was hard and cold,
The wind rushed fiercely at us like a wolf upon the fold;
And we bit our lips and struggled in the terror of the blast,
And we blessed our staffs and wondered if the storm would soon be past.
Sometimes our feet slipped backward on the crusty ice and snow,
Sometimes we stumbled, helpless, for the way was hard to go;
Sometimes we fell, and falling, we were sorry we had tried
To reach the mountain's summit, and the hope within us died.

The path was steep and snowy--the way was hard and cold,
But we struggled ever forward, half afraid--no longer bold;
And with dogged perseverance, we pushed up the hidden trail,
And we seemed but children playing with the elements--too frail
To live long in the displeasure of the wind and hail and sleet,
And the snowy down-like blanket seemed a mammoth winding sheet--
And we almost started homeward with a weary broken sigh,
But we flinched and struggled forward 'neath the scorn that cleft the sky.

The path was steep and snowy--the way was hard and cold,
But at last we reached the summit, and it glittered with the gold
Of the sun that had been shining, with a perfect, glowing light
From behind the heavy storm clouds that had turned the day to night.
And standing on the summit, we looked down and tried to pray,
For we wished to thank the Father who had kept us on our way;
For the snow and sleet and windstorm were but trifles in the past,
And they made the sunshine brighter when we reached the top at last.

--Margaret E. Sangster

IMMORTAL SOUL

O great immortal Soul of mortal man,
God-breathed, ordained to deathless destiny,
Thou, through the ages of eternity,
    Must still live on.

Great minds of philosophical renown
Have fought thy claim to immortality;
Have tried to prove that such could never be
    But all in vain.

God's Word proclaims thy right to endless life,
And proves that death is foreign to thy state;
Let sceptics doubt and men annihilate --
    'Twill not avail.

Some day, 'tis true, thy sojourn here will cease,
This tiny thread of life be snapped in twain,
But thou, O Soul, wilt still alive remain,
    Thou canst not die.

If thou, my Soul, at death couldst cease to be,
What hope could I enjoy? Why was I born?
But there will be a resurrection morn,
    And thou shalt live.

Two destinies are thine, immortal Soul,
But one is endless woe, the other peace;
The choice is thine and life will never cease --
    Which wilt thou choose?

--Oswald J. Smith
Used by permission

"With Thee by faith I walk in crowds--alone,
Making to Thee my wants and wishes known:
Drawing from Thee my daily strength in prayer,
Finding Thine arm sustains me everywhere;
While, thro' the clouds of sin and woe, the light
Of coming glory shines more sweetly bright;
And this my daily boast--my aim--my end--
That my Redeemer is my God--my Friend!"

--C. II. Ironside

WE TWO

"I cannot do it alone;
  The waves run fast and high,
And the fogs close chill around,
  And the light goes out in the sky
But I know that we two shall win--
        in the end;
        --Jesus and I.

"I cannot row it myself--
  The boat on the raging sea--
But beside me sits Another,
  Who pulls or steers--with me;
And I know that we two shall come
        safe into port,
        --His child and He.

"Coward and wayward and weak,
  I change with the changing sky;
Today, so eager and brave,
  Tomorrow, not caring to try;
But He never gives in; so we two
        shall win!
        --Jesus and I.

"Strong and tender and true,
  Crucified once for me;
Ne'er will He change, I know,
  Whatever I may be.
So all He says I should do--
  Ever from sin to keep free;
We shall finish our course, and reach
        Home at last!
        --His child and He."

                              --Selected

  I am far within the mark when I say that all
the armies that ever marched, and all the navies
that ever were built, and all the parliaments
that ever sat, and all the kings that ever reigned,
put together, have not affected the life of man
upon this earth as powerfully as has that one
solitary life--the life of Christ. --Phillips Brooks

MY SOUL THIRSTETH FOR GOD

I thirst, but not as once I did,
The vain delights of earth to share,
Thy wounds, EMMANUEL, all forbid
That I should seek my pleasures there.

It was the sight of Thy dear cross,
First wean'd my soul from earthly things;
And taught me to esteem as dross
The mirth of fools, and pomp of kings.

I want that grace that springs from Thee,
That quickens all things where it flows;
And makes a wretched thorn like me,
Bloom as the myrtle, or the rose.

Dear fountain of delight unknown!
No longer sink below the brim,
But overflow, and pour me down
A living and life-giving stream!

For sure, of all the plants that share
The notice of Thy Father's eye,
None proves less grateful to His care,
Or yields Him meaner fruit than I.

--William Cowper

WATCH YOURSELF GO BY

Just stand aside and watch yourself go by;
Think of yourself as "he," instead of "I."
Note, closely as in other men you note,
The bag-kneed trousers and the seedy coat.
Pick flaws; find fault; forget the man is you,
And strive to make your estimate ring true.
Confront yourself and look you in the eye--
Just stand aside and watch yourself go by.

Interpret all your motives just as though
You looked on one whose aims you did not know.
Let undisguised contempt surge through you when
You see you shirk, O commonest of men!
Despise your cowardice; condemn whate'er
You note of falseness in you anywhere.
Defend not one defect that shames your eye--
Just stand aside and watch yourself go by.

And then, with eyes unveiled to what you loathe--
To sins that with sweet charity you'd clothe--
Back to your self-walled tenement you'll go
With tolerance for all who dwell below.
The faults of others then will dwarf and shrink,
Love's chain grow stronger by one mighty link--
When you, with "he" as substitute for "I,"
Have stood aside and watched yourself go by.

--Strickland Gillilan

INDEX

Index Continued

For a complete list of books available from the Sword of the Lord, write to Sword of the Lord Publishers, P. O. Box 1099, Murfreesboro, Tennessee 37133.